Microsoft®
Access 2016

by Brian Favro

LEVEL 2

LABYRINTH
LEARNING™

Microsoft Access 2016: Level 2

Copyright © 2017 by Labyrinth Learning

LABYRINTH
LEARNING™

Labyrinth Learning
2560 9th Street, Suite 320
Berkeley, California 94710
800.522.9746
On the web at lablearning.com

Product Manager:
Jason Favro

Development Manager:
Laura Popelka

Senior Editor:
Alexandra Mummery

Junior Editor:
Alexandria Henderson

**Assessment and Multimedia
Content Development:**
Ben Linford, Judy Mardar, Andrew
Vaughnley

Production Manager:
Debra Grose

Compositor:
Happenstance Type-O-Rama

Indexer:
Valerie Perry

Interior Design:
Debra Grose

Cover Design:
Mick Koller

ebook only ITEM: 1-59136-872-3
ISBN-13: 978-159136-872-4

ebook with printed textbook ITEM: 1-59136-873-1
ISBN-13: 978-159136-873-1

Manufactured in the United States of America

10 9 8 7 6 5 4 3 2 1

Table of Contents

Preface

This textbook is part of our brand-new approach to learning for introductory computer courses. We've kept the best elements of our proven instructional design and added powerful, interactive elements and assessments that offer enormous potential to engage learners in a new way. We're delighted with the results, and we hope that learners and educators are, too!

Why Did We Write This Content?

In today's digital world, knowing how to use the most common software applications is critical, and those who don't are left behind. Our goal is to simplify the entire learning experience and help every student develop the practical, real-world skills needed to be successful at work and in school. Using a combination of text, videos, interactive elements, and assessments, we begin with fundamental concepts and take learners through a systematic progression of exercises to reach mastery.

What Key Themes Did We Follow?

We had conversations with dozens of educators at community colleges, vocational schools, and other learning environments in preparation for this textbook. We listened and have adapted our learning solution to match the needs of a rapidly changing world, keeping the following common themes in mind:

Keep it about skills. Our content focus is on critical, job-ready topics and tasks, with a relentless focus on practical, real-world skills and common sense as well as step-by-step instruction to ensure that learners stay engaged from the first chapter forward. We've retained our proven method of progressively moving learners through increasingly independent exercises to ensure mastery—an approach that has been successfully developing skills for more than 20 years.

Keep it simple. Our integrated solutions create a seamless and engaging experience built on a uniquely dynamic instructional design that brings clarity to even the most challenging topics. We've focused our content on the things that matter most and have presented it in the easiest way for today's learners to absorb it. Concise chunks of text are combined with visually engaging and interactive elements to increase understanding for all types of learners.

Keep it relevant. Fresh, original, and constantly evolving content helps educators keep pace with today's student and work environments. We have reviewed every topic for relevancy and have updated it where needed to offer realistic examples and projects for learners.

How Do I Use This Book?

We understand that we are in a time of transition and that some students will still appreciate a print textbook to support their learning. Our comprehensive learning solution consists of a groundbreaking interactive ebook for primary content delivery and our easy-to-use eLab course management tool for assessment. We want to help students as they transition to a digital solution. Our interactive ebook contains learning content delivered in ways that will engage learners. Students can utilize a print text supplement in conjunction with the ebook that provides all the textual elements from the ebook in a full-color, spiral-bound print format.

Our eLab platform provides additional learning content such as overviews for each chapter, automatically graded projects and other assessments that accurately assess student skills, and clear feedback and analytics on student actions.

Included with Your Textbook Purchase

▶ *Interactive ebook*: A dynamic, engaging, and truly interactive textbook that includes elements such as videos, self-assessments, slide shows, and other interactive features. Highlighting, taking notes, and searching for content is easy.

▶ *eLab Course Management System*: A robust tool for accurate assessment, tracking of learner activity, and automated grading that includes a comprehensive set of instructor resources. eLab can be fully integrated with your LMS, making course management even easier.

▶ *Instructor resources*: This course is also supported on the Labyrinth website with a comprehensive instructor support package that includes detailed lesson plans, PowerPoint presentations, a course syllabus, test banks, additional exercises, and more.

▶ *Learning Resource Center*: The exercise files that accompany this textbook can be found within eLab and on the Learning Resource Center, which may be accessed from the ebook or online at: **www.labyrinthelab.com/lrc**.

▶ *Overview chapter content*: The "Overview Chapter ISM" folder in the Instructor Support Materials package and the "Overview Chapter Files" folder in the Student Exercise File download include the helpful "Introducing Microsoft Office and Using Common Features" chapter. In addition to providing a discussion of the various Office versions, this chapter introduces a selection of features common throughout the Office applications. **We recommend that students complete this "overview" chapter first.**

We're excited to share this innovative, new approach with you, and we'd love you to share your experience with us at www.lablearning.com/share.

Display Settings

Multiple factors, including screen resolution, monitor size, and window size, can affect the appearance of the Microsoft Ribbon and its buttons. In this textbook, screen captures were taken at the native (recommended) screen resolutions in Office 2016 running Windows 10, with ClearType enabled.

Visual Conventions

This book uses visual and typographic cues to guide students through the lessons. Some of these cues are described below.

Cue Name	What It Does
`Type this text`	Text you type at the keyboard is printed in this typeface.
Action words	The important action words in exercise steps are presented in boldface.
Ribbon	Glossary terms are highlighted with a light yellow background.
Note! Tip! Warning!	Tips, notes, and warnings are called out with special icons.
	Videos and WebSims that are a required part of this course are indicated by this icon.
Command→Command→ Command→Command	Commands to execute from the Ribbon are presented like this: Ribbon Tab→Command Group→Command→Subcommand.
≡ **Design→Themes→Themes**	These notes present shortcut steps for executing certain tasks.

Acknowledgements

Many individuals contribute to the development and completion of a textbook. We appreciate the careful attention and informed contributions of Carol Rogers, Accounting Program Chair at Central New Mexico Community College, and Rick Street, Spokane Community College, for their assistance in the development of this book.

We are also deeply grateful to the instructors and professionals who reviewed the text and suggested improvements.

This book has benefited significantly from the feedback and suggestions of the following reviewers:

Pam Silvers, *Asheville-Buncombe Technical Community College*

Ramiro Villareal, *Brookhaven College*

Teresa Loftis, *Inland Career Education Center*

Kim Pigeon, *Northeast Wisconsin Technical College*

Lynne Kemp, *North Country Community College*

Tom Martin, *Shasta College*

Karen LaPlant, *Hennepin Technical College*

Kay Gerken, *College of DuPage*

Colleen Kennedy, *Spokane Community College*

5

Refining Table Design

It's important to understand what makes Access a relational database management system and why properly designed databases perform better. Well-designed databases reduce redundant data and create critical connections between the objects that help make them more efficient to use. In this chapter, you will develop important table relationships and use tools to help speed data entry and ensure data accuracy.

LEARNING OBJECTIVES

▸ Create and modify relationships

▸ Format a table datasheet layout

▸ Modify table structure

▸ Set field properties

▸ Use the Lookup Wizard

📂 Project: Maintaining and Formatting Databases

You are tasked with maintaining the Winchester Web Design database. After reviewing the objects in the database, you decide to make some changes that will make the database more efficient and improve data entry. You will create a lookup field to streamline data entry. In the process, you will add some formatting to make the tables more colorful. You will then examine the relationships between tables to ensure that they define the database accurately.

Creating and Modifying Relationships

As you build tables and other objects in a relational database, Access creates some of the relationships between tables based upon the field structure of each table. However, it's a good idea to examine and edit these relationships manually. For example, you may choose to cascade updated or deleted records; that is, to automatically update or delete all affected records as part of a single operation. Cascade options can be invaluable in cases where a store pulls a product off of its shelf, and therefore needs to remove that product from its merchandise list, order list, inventory list, and advertising list. And in most cases, you also must enforce referential integrity to ensure that relationships between records in related tables are valid. Finally, it may be wise to create and display those relationships in a report to add to the database documentation.

Relationship Types

Database relationships connect data in one table to data stored in other tables. Access supports three different types of relationships:

▶ A one-to-one relationship means that each record in Table A can have only one matching record in Table B, and each record in Table B can have only one matching record in Table A. This is the least common relationship. A good example is a main Customers table linked to a CustPassword table. One customer has one password.

▶ A one-to-many relationship means that each record in Table A can have multiple matching records in Table B, but a record in Table B can have only one matching record in Table A. This is the most common relationship. Here's an example: One employee will have many sales, and a product will be sold many times.

▶ A many-to-many relationship occurs when two tables may each have many matches in the other table, but they do not share key fields, so they use a third junction table to tie the two tables together to complete the relationship. The junction table has a one-to-many relationship to each table. An example is a vendors table and a products table, where one vendor provides many different products and one product is available from many vendors.

Adding, Deleting, and Modifying Relationships

There are times when a database designer must add, delete, or change a relationship. To modify tables after relationships have been set, you must temporarily delete existing relationships so Access is free to make the revisions without violating integrity rules. For example, say you have an existing Short Text data type field, such as State, and you want to change it to a Lookup data type. If you attempt to change its data type, Access will display a warning message indicating that you must first delete its relationships to any other tables. After you delete the relationship and change the field's data type, you may have to reestablish the relationship and edit those relationship properties.

Referential Integrity Requirements

Perhaps the most important database relationship protocol is referential integrity, which is a set of rules used to maintain the validity of the related data in a database. It ensures that you don't delete a record or change a primary key that is related to data in a foreign table. It also requires the data types of the related fields (both the primary and foreign keys) to be the same or compatible.

Referential integrity is a critical part of a relational database, so let's look at it from several different views using real-life examples:

▶ If the ProdID primary key in the Products table has a Number data type (that is, Field Size property: Long Integer), then the ProdID foreign key in the Invoice Details table must also have the Number data type (that is, Field Size property: Long Integer).

▶ You cannot have a listing in the Invoice Details table for a product that you don't sell. This means that you cannot have a foreign key (that is, ProdID) in the Invoice Details table without a matching primary key (that is, ProdID) in the Products table.

▶ You cannot delete the primary key (that is, ProdID) from the Products table when there is a corresponding foreign key (that is, ProdID) in the Invoice Details table.

▶ You cannot change the primary key value (that is, 01HP) from the Products table when there is an existing and corresponding foreign key value (that is, 01HP) in the Invoice Details table, unless Cascade Update is enabled.

Relationship Cascade Options

Two additional relationship options are available so that you can control updates to related tables: Cascade Update and Cascade Delete. Each has a unique function for maintaining database relationships, and it's important to know what they control before using them.

RELATIONSHIP CASCADE OPTIONS

Cascade Option	Description
Cascade Update	Updates the value in the key field of a related table if you change the primary key value in the primary table. For example, if you change a ProdID in the Products table, the ProdID field value in the Invoice Details table updates for each invoice.
Cascade Delete	Deletes records in a related table any time you delete related records in the primary table. You might consider this option if you deleted an employee from the Employees table and want to also delete their spouse from the Spouses table. However, use this option with caution because it would not be wise to delete all 2012 invoice records for an employee just because that employee retired in 2013.

ACCESS

The Edit Relationships Box

You can examine, create, and edit relationships between tables in the Relationships window. To create relationships manually, use the Edit Relationships box to identify the rules you want Access to enforce.

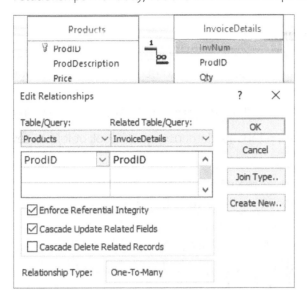

Notice the one-to-many relationship join line between the ProdID fields, which indicates that referential integrity has been enforced.

≡ Database Tools→Relationships→Relationships ⊟

DEVELOP YOUR SKILLS: A5-D1

In this exercise, you will open the Relationships window, add a table, and create a relationship between tables. You will also set referential integrity for the relationship.

Before You Begin: *Be sure to visit the Learning Resource Center at labyrinthelab.com/lrc to retrieve the exercise files for this course before beginning this exercise.*

1. Open **A5-D1-WinWebDesign** from your **Access Chapter 5** folder and save it as **A5-D1-WinWebDesignRevised**.

   When completing exercises, always choose to Enable Content.

2. Choose **Database Tools→Relationships→Relationships** ⊟.

3. Click the **Show Table** ⊞ button.

4. Double-click the **EmpSpouses** and **All_Customers** tables to add them to the Relationships window and then close the Show Table box.

   Typically, all tables will be in the Relationships window, but sometimes tables are added at a later time.

5. Rearrange the tables within the Relationships window by dragging their title bars until they are arranged as shown below.

   Arranging the tables in this manner will help you see all the relationships, as the relationship lines are not overlapping.

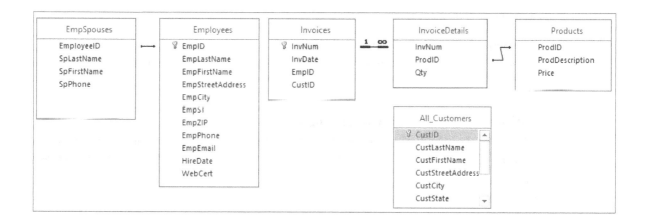

Manually Set Relationships

Now you will create a one-to-many relationship between the Employees table and the Invoices table so one employee may have many invoices.

6. Follow these steps to create a relationship between the Employees and Invoices tables:

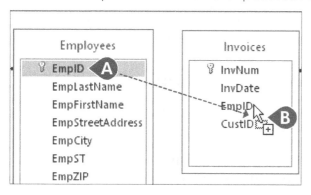

    A   Select the EmpID field in the Employees table and drag it to the **EmpID** field in the Invoices table.

    B   When the mouse pointer is positioned as shown, release the mouse button.

    The Edit Relationships dialog box opens once the mouse button is released.

7. Check the **Enforce Referential Integrity** box and click **Create**.

    Access places symbols at each end of the join line. The Employees end of the join line displays a 1 and the Orders end displays an infinity sign (∞).

8. Drag the **CustID** primary key from the All_Customers table to the **CustID** field in the Invoices table.

9. Enforce referential integrity and click **Create** to complete the relationship.

10. Choose **File→Save** or click the **Save** button to save the database changes and leave the Relationships window open.

 Keep Access and any databases or database objects being used open at the end of each exercise unless instructed to close them.

ACCESS

Editing Relationships

Setting cascade options can have a ripple effect on records and data in a database. So it's a good idea to back up a database before setting these options and then test the settings. That way you can restore the database from the backup if the changes you make to the settings result in data loss.

When to Review Relationships

Any time the structure of a table changes—whether it's through adding or removing fields, changing data types, or creating lookup fields—you should review and update the relationships among database tables.

DEVELOP YOUR SKILLS: A5-D2

In this exercise, you will edit the relationship between the Employees and Invoices tables so that if you change the Employee ID in the primary table (Employees), Access will update the Employee ID in the related foreign table (Invoices).

1. Right-click the **join line** between the Employees table and the Invoices table and choose **Edit Relationships**.

   The mouse pointer must be right on the join line or you won't see the Edit Relationships option on the right-click menu.

2. Check the **Cascade Update Related Fields** checkbox and click **OK**.

3. Choose **File→Save** or click the **Save** button to save the relationship change.

Documenting and Printing Relationships

After you have inspected the relationships, you may want to create a report to view a printable version of the relationships. You can also display the database objects that make use of, or are used by, other objects in the database. This is done through the Object Dependencies panel.

≡ Database Tools→Relationships→Relationships→Relationship Report 🖼

≡ Database Tools→Relationships→Object Dependencies 🖼

DEVELOP YOUR SKILLS: A5-D3

In this exercise, you will create a relationship report and examine object dependencies for the Employees table.

1. In the Relationships window, if necessary, move the All_Customers table slightly, and any other tables as necessary, until all join lines are clearly visible.

2. Choose **Design→Tools→Relationship Report** 🖼.

3. Choose **File→Save** or click the **Save** button and save the report as **Relationships**.

   The report is added to the Report group in the Navigation pane.

4. Close the report and then close the Relationships window.

5. Click (but don't open) the **Employees** table in the Navigation pane.

6. Choose **Database Tools→Relationships→Object Dependencies** 🗔.

7. Review the Objects That Depend on Me option in the Object Dependencies panel

   Many objects—other tables, queries, forms, and reports—depend on the Employees table.

8. Choose the **Objects That I Depend On** option.

   The Employees table has relationships with, or depends on, the EmpSpouses, Invoices, and States tables.

9. Close the Object Dependencies panel.

Modifying Table Structures

Database integrity and data validity are important aspects of database maintenance. Access offers a number of features that enable you to modify table fields, control the data entered, and format the data to ensure consistent reporting. These features include, but are not limited to:

▶ Renaming tables, forms, and other database objects

▶ Adding and removing fields from tables

▶ Changing data types

Renaming Tables and Editing, Adding, and Deleting Table Fields

As you create tables, you define each field by setting the data type and entering the field name. Access works behind the scenes and sets default properties for the field that limit the number of characters in a field, as well as the format and data type of characters that are valid for the field. You can accept the default properties Access sets or modify the properties. Properties available depend on the data type selected for the field. Care must be taken when adding, editing, or deleting fields because of the impact such actions might have on the table data.

Renaming Tables

When you save a table, give it a name that describes the data it contains. You can later change the name without affecting its data. However, note that table names are often included in other database objects that use the table's data. So, renaming a table can impact other database objects. If you rename a table, make sure that every form, query, or report that uses that table still works.

Traditionally, it was wise to *not* include spaces in table names because referencing the table in a query could be confusing. For instance—is *Invoice Details* two objects or one object? Fortunately, Access will enclose a table name like *Invoice Details* within square brackets ([ ]) when it uses it in an expression.

Adding Fields to Existing Tables

Periodically you will need to create new fields in existing database tables and then add data to these fields. You can add a field either in Datasheet View or in Table Design View and then move it where you want it to be in the layout.

Deleting Fields

When you delete a field that contains data, Access displays a message warning you that deleting the field will remove all its data. If you delete a field in Design View and have not saved the table, you can recover the deleted field using the Undo command. If, however, you save the table after deleting the field, the data is lost and you have to add the field name to the Table Design and then reenter all field data in the table to restore the data. Fields are deleted in Design View by clicking the field header and tapping Delete.

Editing Field Data Types

Many Access data types start with a different letter, which means you can type a letter and the data type that begins with that letter will display. For example, if you want to change the data type of a field from Short Text to Number, you click in the field's Data Type and type **N**.

Any time you change the data type of a field that contains values that fail to conform to the new data type, Access deletes any nonconforming data. For example, if you change a field's data type from Short Text to a Number data type and someone has accidentally entered *1O* (using a capital *O*) instead of *10* (using zero), Access will warn you that you are about to delete data that did not conform. The great thing about this is that Access will only allow valid field data, which results in more accurate data.

The Yes/No Data Type

The Yes/No data type sets the field so that only two entries are possible—Yes/No, True/False, or On/Off. When you set the Yes/No data type for a field, Access places a checkbox for the field in the datasheet and on forms where the data appears. Checking the checkbox indicates a value of Yes, True, On, etc.; clearing the checkbox indicates a value of No, False, or Off.

DEVELOP YOUR SKILLS: A5-D4

In this exercise, you will rename a table, delete a table field, add a table field, and modify the data type of a field.

1. Right-click the **All_Customers** table in the Navigation pane and choose **Rename**.
2. Type **Customers** and tap Enter.
3. Open the **Customers** table and switch to **Design View**.
4. Click the **field selection** box on the left edge of the Notes field to select the field.

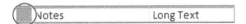

5. Tap Delete and choose **Yes** to confirm the deletion.

   The field, and any data contained within the field, have been permanently removed from the database. However, you could use Undo to restore the field and data because you made the deletion while working in Design View.

Add New Fields

Now you will add a Yes/No field to the Customers table.

6. Right-click the **CustStreetAddress** field selection box and choose **Insert Rows**.

   A new row opens above the CustStreetAddress row.

7. Click in the empty **Field Name** box of your new field and type **Business** as the name.

8. Tap ⌷Tab⌷ and set the Data Type to **Yes/No**.

9. Choose **File→Save** or click the **Save** button to save the table.

10. Switch to **Datasheet View**.

    Notice your new Yes/No Business field has all boxes unchecked (that is, set to No).

11. Check the **Business** field boxes for the records with the following CustIDs: **DavisP**, **HassanA**, and **KleinJ**.

    These records are now identified as having a business.

12. Close the Customers table.

Formatting a Table Datasheet Layout

It's difficult to plan and prepare for all of the possibilities that may occur as a database is first developed. For instance, if field values are longer than anticipated, Access will display only the portion of the data that fits within the column width, causing some of the data to be unseen. Or the opposite scenario may occur, in which one or two fields were added, and you need to display all the fields on one screen, which means that you may have to modify the width of each column to fit the screen. Alternatively, you can maximize the Access window or close the Navigation pane to provide more room without having to modify the width of each column.

Changing the Width of Columns

Access offers some useful techniques to adjust the width of each column in a datasheet to display all data in the column:

▸ **Drag a column border:** Drag a column border to make the column on the left of the border wider or narrower.

▸ **Double-click a column heading border:** Double-click the right border of a column to change the width of the column on the left to fit either the longest data entry in the column or column heading, whichever is wider.

▸ **Right-click a field heading and choose Field Width:** Select the Field Width command from the context menu to open the Column Width dialog box and type the width, reset the standard width, or select Best Fit to automatically size the field width to the longest entry.

Moving and Hiding Data Columns

There will be times when you want to reposition a column of data in a table layout—perhaps to display the email address before the telephone number. When you rearrange the columns in a datasheet, the table layout remains the same but the fields display in a different order in the datasheet. You may also want to hide some columns so you can better view other field columns. When you hide columns, Access temporarily removes them from display. The data, however, remains in the table—it is not deleted. If you want to view data in hidden columns at a later time, you unhide the column.

Saving a Table Layout

Changing the layout of a table datasheet has no real effect on table data or structure; however, when you make changes to a table datasheet, Access recognizes the differences between the structure of the table and its layout, and prompts you to save the changes to the layout when you close the table. If you abandon the changes, the next time you open the table datasheet, the column widths will return to their original size and any columns that were hidden will show. If you save the changes, the next time you open the table datasheet, Access recalls the layout and displays the formatting changes.

DEVELOP YOUR SKILLS: A5-D5

In this exercise, you will adjust column width to allow for the best display of data in a datasheet, rearrange columns, and hide a column.

1. Display the **Customers** table in **Datasheet View**.

2. Position the mouse pointer between the Street Address and City column headings and double-click when the adjust pointer appears as shown here.

   The Street Address column width will adjust to fit the widest entry in the column.

3. Position the mouse pointer on the **CustID** column heading and drag right until both the CustID and Last Name columns are selected as shown here. Release the mouse button.

   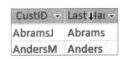

4. Position the mouse pointer between the column headings and double–click when the adjust pointer appears.

   Both columns will be Best Fit.

5. Click the **First Name** column heading to select the column.

6. Drag the **First Name** column to the left of the Last Name column and release the mouse button when the black vertical bar is positioned as shown here.

   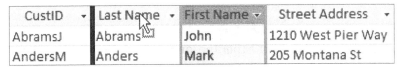

   First Name should now be before Last Name.

7. Click the table selection button to select all data as shown here.

   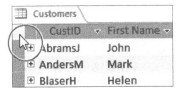

8. Double-click the border between any of the selected column headings to Best Fit all columns.

9. Close the Customers table, saving your changes.

Enhancing a Datasheet

Changing the datasheet layout enables you to make necessary adjustments, such as widening a field so that a longer value can be fully displayed. Enhancing the datasheet layout enables you to improve its readability. Some of the features you can apply to enhance a datasheet include gridlines, font size and color, and background color.

As you apply enhancements to the datasheet, Access formats all data and gridlines to match the format you choose. The Text Formatting group on the Home tab displays tools for enhancing the most commonly formatted features on a datasheet such as fonts, colors, fills, and alignments. And it also contains tools for formatting alternate rows and gridlines. Finally, a Datasheet Formatting dialog box can be launched from the Text Formatting group from which additional datasheet formatting can be applied.

Gridline formatting

Alternate row formatting

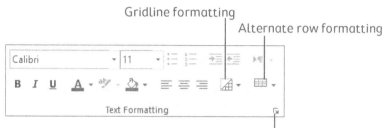

Dialog box launcher opens the Datasheet Formatting box

☰ Home→Text Formatting

DEVELOP YOUR SKILLS: A5-D6

In this exercise, you will use the Text Formatting tools to set datasheet enhancement options for the Customers table.

1. Open the **Customers** table in **Datasheet View**.
2. Choose **Home→Text Formatting→Alternate Row Color** ⊞ **menu button** ▼.
3. Choose the **Blue, Accent 1** color, which is the 5th color on the top row of Theme Colors.

   Alternate rows in the datasheet should now be blue.
4. Choose **Home→Text Formatting→Font menu button** ▼ and choose **Arial** from the font list.

   All table data should now be formatted with the Arial font.
5. Choose **Home→Text Formatting→Gridlines** ▦ **menu button** ▼ and choose **Gridlines: Horizontal**.

   The datasheet will only display horizontal gridlines now.
6. Click the **Home→Text Formatting** group dialog box launcher as shown below to open the Datasheet Formatting dialog box.

7. Click the **Gridline Color menu** button ▼ and choose **Black, Text 1** (2nd color on the top row of Theme Colors).
8. Click **OK** to apply the black gridlines.
9. Choose **File→Save** and save the changes to the Customers table.

Setting Field Properties

Field properties are settings that enable you to further define the properties of each field. The Field Properties pane appears in the lower portion of the Table Design View or on the Fields tab in Datasheet View. The most frequently used properties are identified in the following table.

COMMON FIELD PROPERTIES

Field Property	Description
Field Size	Sets a field length for the number of characters each field can hold.
Format	Sets a predefined display layout for fields (that is, currency or percent).
Input Mask	Identifies the format of values entered—with hyphens or without, alphabetic or numeric, uppercase or lowercase, etc.
Caption	Sets a column heading title to describe the data content better than the actual field name. Includes spaces where appropriate.
Default Value	Adds a default value for a specific field in each record, such as FL for the State field, abbreviated as "ST."
Validation Rule	Controls actual values entered into a field, such as less than 100 or greater than 01/01/2017.
Validation Text	Provides a tip that identifies valid data entries, such as "All dates must be after 01/01/2017."
Required	Sets the field as required to ensure a value is entered in the field.

Why Set Field Properties?

Different people add data to databases—and they often enter the data differently. For example, some people type parentheses around the area code when entering phone numbers. Others may separate the area code from the number using a hyphen. Both formats are accurate, but displaying mismatched data can be distracting. Entering parentheses or hyphens can also be time-consuming. Setting field properties to control how data appears helps maintain data consistency throughout a database.

Set Field Sizes, Captions, and Default Values

Maintaining database integrity, data validity, and data format are important considerations when building a database. You should make every effort to ensure that data is entered consistently, contains the required number of characters, and falls within valid data ranges.

Setting Field Size

Rather than using a default field size, you can set the Field Size property to limit the number of characters that can be entered into the field for each record. For example, you can limit data entry of state names to the two-character state abbreviation.

Sometimes, when you reduce an existing field size to limit data entry, Access displays a warning that data may be lost due to the reduced field size. In most cases, you are familiar with the data, so you can choose *Yes* to continue. For instance, truncating Florida to FL would not create invalid data. However, if you are uncertain, you should choose *No*, check the data to ensure that it fits the new limit, and then set the field size.

Identifying Field Size for Number Fields

Number fields are identified by special formats in the Properties panel. In general, number fields should be set to define the largest value anticipated for the field. Setting the proper field size controls for number fields helps optimize database performance. The following table identifies each Number field format and describes the type of data each stores.

NUMBER FIELD FORMATS	
Field Size Property	**Description**
Byte	Stores whole numbers between 0 and 255 using one byte and allows no fractions or decimal points; uses the minimum amount of memory, allowing for the fastest processing.
Integer	Stores whole numbers between –32,768 and 32,767 using 2 bytes rather than the standard 7 bytes normally used for high values.
Long Integer	Stores whole numbers between –2,147,483,648 and 2,147,483,647 using 4 bytes rather than the standard 14 bytes normally used for high values.
Single	Stores positive and negative numbers to exactly seven decimal places using 4 bytes.
Double	Stores positive and negative numbers to exactly 15 decimal places using 8 bytes.
Replication ID	Identifies replication of tables, records, and other objects in Access 2003 or earlier databases using 16 bytes.
Decimal	Stores positive and negative numbers to exactly 28 decimal places using 12 bytes.

Setting Text to Uppercase or Lowercase Format

Text fields have unique field properties available for formatting data. Access provides a Format field that enables you to force a specific format to all characters in the field. The most common format characters are used to force uppercase (>) and lowercase (<). Using the Text Format property eliminates the need to spend valuable time entering multiple characters in the Input Mask property.

Setting Captions

As you may have noticed, many field names contain no spaces or include an underscore, such as LastName or Last_Name. The Caption field property enables you to type a more descriptive name for a field that is more suitable for display on forms, in datasheets, and on reports—such as Last Name.

Setting Default Field Values

Validation rules control the data you enter in table fields. Setting a default value for a field automatically enters the most common data value and can save time and help reduce the number of errors made during data entry.

For instance, all the employees at Winchester Web Design live in Florida. Consequently, it saves time and reduces inconsistency when the default value for the State field is set to FL. The default value appears whenever a new record is added. If you need to enter a different state, you simply type in the new state's two-character abbreviation to replace the default value.

Making a Field Required

Whenever you create a primary key field, its properties are automatically set to be required and indexed, allowing no duplicates. A database index is a structure whose main function is to speed up database operations. An index that is set on key fields enables faster searches and retrieval of data.

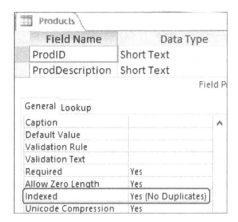

A key field must have a value; by default, every other field does not require that a value be entered. There are times, however, when non-key fields must have values. For instance, you must include an employee last name and first name when entering a new record into your Employees table. The Required field property helps to easily accomplish this.

DEVELOP YOUR SKILLS: A5-D7

In this exercise, you will set field sizes, captions, and default values in the Customers table.

1. If necessary, open the **Customers** table and switch to **Design View**.

2. Click anywhere in the **CustState** field and set the following Field Properties:

   Field Size: **2**
   Format: **>**
   Caption: **ST**
   Default Value: **FL**

   Entering > for the Format property converts entries to uppercase. Access places quotation marks around the Default Value field property when you click in another field property or save the table. Setting field sizes that are consistent with the data they hold helps the data display properly when it's included in forms and reports.

3. Click anywhere in the **CustLastName** field and change the field size to **25** and the required property to **Yes**.

4. Click anywhere in the **CustPhone** field and change the field size to **15** and the required property to **Yes**.

5. Choose **File→Save**, choose **Yes** when the Some Data May Be Lost message appears, and choose **Yes** again when the Data Integrity Rules Have Been Changed message appears.

6. Switch to **Datasheet View** and enter this data in a new record:

Field	Data to Enter
CustID	**JonesK**
First Name	**Ken**
Last Name	Leave this field blank.
Business	Check the box to set it to **Yes**.
Street Address	**2300 Maple Ave.**
City	**Palmetto**
ST	This field will already be set to FL, as you set FL as the default value.
ZIP	**34628**
Telephone	Leave this field blank.
Email	**KJones@email.com**

7. Tap Tab after entering the email address and you will be prompted to enter a value for the Customers.CustLastName field, because you made it a required field.

8. Click **OK** and then type **Jones** in the Last Name field.

9. Tap Tab repeatedly until you are prompted to enter a value for the Customers.CustPhone field, since it is also a required field.

10. Click **OK** and then enter **9415553232** as the telephone number, tapping Tab when you are finished.

Access automatically applies parentheses, ( ), to the area code and a hyphen, -, after 555.

Custom Text and Memo Field Formats

Standard field formats in Access cannot meet the needs of every text or memo field contained in every database. That's why Access provides tools for creating custom formats. Custom formats for Text and Memo fields can contain two sections:

▸ **Section 1:** Contains a symbol and is followed by a semicolon when a second section is entered.

▸ **Section 2:** Contains the value of the alternate value when no value is entered. This alternate is a *null* value and is enclosed in quotation marks with no space between: "".

An example of a two-section format for a text field would look like this: @; "N/A"

The @ symbol tells Access to display the field data if a value is entered, and N/A tells Access to display N/A (Not Applicable) if no value is entered. The @ symbol displays all the characters that will fit the Field Size property, and if there are fewer characters than the Field Size value, Access pads the rest of the field with blank spaces.

Short Text and Long Text Field Unique Properties

Text and Memo fields are formatted to hold text characters (abc), symbols (#$%), and numbers (123) on which no mathematical calculations will be performed, such as FirstName, LastName, City, and also ZipCode, PhoneNumber, and SocSecNumber. Because of the broad scope of data that these data types can contain, Access provides several field properties for controlling and formatting data entry in the field.

SHORT TEXT AND LONG TEXT FIELD UNIQUE PROPERTIES	
Property	**Description**
Allow Zero Length	Allows data entry of zero length in a field. Data is entered as open and close parentheses with no character or space between: (). The purpose of this entry is to show that there is no value to enter. For example, if you have a field in a Customers table that requires a land phone number and the customer has no land phone, you would enter () in the field.
Text Format	This property will set the text in a Long Text field as Plain Text or Rich Text. Rich text fields can be formatted with different fonts, font sizes, and colors.
Text Align	Positions the text on the left, center, or right side of the field box or column. The Distribute setting spreads out the text to fill the column or text box size.
Append Only	Adds a series of date-stamped comments to a single Long Text field, making it easy to create a history log of comments added to the fields. These comments are stored in a separate table and accessed through the Append Only Long Text field.

Entering Field Properties

Access provides three basic techniques for setting field properties:

▶ Type the value into the property box.

▶ Choose the value from the property list. (For example, click the drop-down menu button to select a valid entry from the list.)

▶ Click the Build button that appears at the right side of a field property to open the Wizard associated with that property. Then choose the settings you want to apply. For example, click the Build button to open the Input Mask Wizard to format the display of text and field dates.

DEVELOP YOUR SKILLS: A5-D8

In this exercise, you will set additional properties to require the entry of a customer's first name.

1. Display the **Customers** table in **Design View**.

2. Click anywhere in the **CustFirstName** field and type **@** for the Format field property.

   Using the @ symbol will display all characters that fit within the field size and pad any remaining positions with spaces.

3. Choose **Yes** in the Required field property and **No** in the Allow Zero Length field property to prohibit a null value from being entered.

   These settings will require a CustFirstName to always be entered.

4. Choose **File→Save** or click the **Save** button and choose **Yes** when advised that the data integrity rules have been changed.

5. Switch to **Datasheet View**.

6. Click in the **CustID** field of the new, blank record at the bottom of the table and type **SmithA**.

7. Type **Smith** in the Last Name field and then close the Customers table.

   A message appears informing you that you must enter a value in the CustFirstName field. This is because you set the Allow Zero Length property to No, which requires an entry of at least one character to be made.

8. Click **OK** to dismiss the message and then click **Yes** to close the database object (the table) now.

   The table will close and the new record you started to enter will not be saved.

Formatting Data Using Input Masks

Consistency of data format is important for visual aesthetics; it also helps ensure accuracy in searches, queries, and sorts. You can control data formats using the field property input mask. Using input masks, you can set the characters you want displayed in fields, such as the parentheses in an area code, and Access requires the user to enter the data within that format.

The Input Mask Wizard

The Input Mask Wizard is a valuable tool for setting the most common formats used in databases. You can also set input masks to require a specific number of characters in a field or to convert characters to capital or lowercase.

Setting input masks ensures that the data format in tables is consistent. Because the table data is consistent, data displayed in forms and reports will also be consistent.

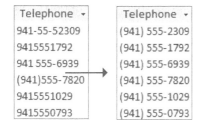

Input masks can automatically format unformatted data.

A Build ••• button appears at the right end of the Input Mask box when you click the box. It starts the Input Mask Wizard, which helps you build the mask.

Input Mask Symbols

When you use the Input Mask Wizard, Access places the necessary coding into the Field Properties pane. Access uses several symbols to control the appearance of data.

Symbol	Description	Example
0	Requires a numeric digit	(000) 000-0000 requires an area code as part of the phone number.
9	Data is optional but must be a digit	(999) 000-0000 requires a seven-digit phone number with an optional three-digit area code.
#	Restricts data to a digit, +, -, or space	#99.99 permits + or – in the position of the #.
L	Requires an alphabetic character (that is, a letter)	LL requires the entry of two alphabetic characters in the State field.
?	Restricts, but does not require, data to alphabetic characters	L????L requires two alphabetic characters, one on each end of the data, but permits four additional alphabetic characters in between.
A	Requires an alphabetic or numeric character	000-AAAA permits a phone number to be entered either as 555-1234 or 555-HOME.
a	Allows, but does not require, alphabetic or numeric characters	(aaa) AAA-AAAA requires a seven-digit phone number but not the area code.
&	Requires any alphanumeric character (a letter or a number) or a space	&&&& permits data entry such as a four-character ID such as 01HP, 1 HP, or 1234.
C	Allows, but does not require, any character or space	CCCC could contain an entry such as 01HP, 1 HP, HP, etc.
.,:;-/	Characters used to separate parts of numeric, date, time, and currency values	#,###.## permits numeric data. 99/99/00 permits date data. 99:00:00 permits time date.
<	Converts characters to lowercase	<aaa permits entry of three characters such as *ABC* and converts data to lowercase *abc*.
>	Converts characters to uppercase	>aa permits entry of two characters such as *fl* and converts the data to *FL*.
!	Displays input mask characters from right to left	!(#) 000-0000 right-aligns the phone number so that if only seven numbers are entered, the area code is left blank. This affects fields defined with the Number data type.
\	Causes characters that follow the \ to display as literal characters	(\A) appears as (A).
"Literal Text"	Places text that appears between the quotation marks into the field value at the identified position	"ID-"0000 places *ID-* before the numbers entered. A space may be enclosed in quotes to ensure it appears in the value.
Password	Creates a password entry text box. Any character typed in the text box is stored as a character but displays as an asterisk (*) as the password is entered	When passWord1! is typed, Access shows **********.

Storing Input Mask Characters

Access provides two methods for storing the input mask with the table data—with or without the symbols. Storing the symbols with the data increases the size of the database file. Therefore, companies that store extremely large volumes of data often prefer storing the data without the input mask symbols. You can choose one of these methods while running the Input Mask Wizard.

Using Smart Tags

As you work in Access, you will periodically see smart tags, such as the Paste Options smart tag, which you may have seen in Word and other Microsoft applications. Smart tags allow you to apply formatting changes you make to a field in one table to the same field anywhere else it occurs in the database. For example, if you modify the field format properties in a table, the Property Options smart tag lets you apply the same format changes to the field when it appears in other forms, queries, and reports. This helps ensure the consistency of data throughout the database.

DEVELOP YOUR SKILLS: A5-D9

In this exercise, you will set the primary key, change a field size, and apply a custom input mask to a field in the Products table. Then you will apply a standard telephone input mask to a field in the Employees table.

1. Open the **Products** table in **Datasheet View**.

   Notice the ProdID field consists of two numeric characters and two alphabetic characters.

2. Switch to **Design View** and click the **Primary Key** 🔑 button to make **ProdID** the primary key field.

3. Click in the **Input Mask** field properties box and type **"PROD-"00AA** (use zeros not the letter O for 00).

   This input mask formats the ProdID field to automatically begin with PROD- followed by 2 numbers and then 2 letters.

4. Choose **File→Save** or click the **Save** button, and the Property Update Options smart tag will appear next to the input mask you just entered.

5. Click the **smart tag** 🗐 and choose **Update Input Mask Everywhere ProdID Is Used**.

   Access displays the Update Properties dialog box, which contains a list of all objects using the field. For this field, only one object is listed.

6. Click **Yes** to update the Products Report object.

7. Switch to **Datasheet View**.

   Notice the ProdID field now has PROD- preceding each product ID.

8. Close the Products table.

Use the Input Mask Wizard

Now you will apply a standard input mask format to a field.

9. Open the **Employees** table in **Datasheet View**.

   Notice the Telephone field contains numbers without any other symbols.

10. Switch to **Design View** and click anywhere in the **EmpPhone** field.

11. Click in the **Input Mask** field property box and then click the ⋯ button on the right side of the box.

12. Choose **Phone Number** as the input mask and click **Finish**.

13. Choose **File→Save** to save the table and then switch to **Datasheet View**.

   Notice the phone numbers are now formatted with parentheses and a hyphen because of the input mask.

14. Switch back to **Design View**

Create Additional Settings

15. Change these field properties to set the field sizes, input masks, and captions shown below.

   Note that for both the EmpLastName and EmpFirstName input masks you should use 24 question marks (?), and you should use 14 question marks ? for the EmpCity input mask. These input masks use the >L< symbols to specify that the first character should automatically be capitalized, and the next 24 or 14 questions marks ? specify that up to 24 or 14 alphabetic characters can be entered.

Field	Field Size	Input Mask	Caption
EmpLastName	25	>L<????????????????????????	Last Name
EmpFirstName	25	>L<????????????????????????	First Name
EmpStreetAddress	30		Street Address
EmpCity	15	>L<??????????????	City
EmpST	2	>LL	State
EmpZIP			ZIP
EmpEmail			Email
HireDate			Hire Date
WebCert			Web Cert

16. Choose **File→Save** or click the **Save** button and choose **Yes** when advised that some data may be lost.

17. Switch to **Datasheet View**.

   Notice the column headings now show the captions rather than the field names. The Caption property lets you use descriptive headings for fields, as field names cannot contain spaces.

18. Close the Employees table.

Setting Validation Rules

A validation rule is a field property that enables you to limit the values entered into the field in order to reduce inaccurate data entry. You could, for example, set a validation rule to limit the value typed into an HoursWorked field to fifty or fewer, or the value of Pay Rate to less than $60.

Setting Appropriate Data Types for Validation Rules

For validation rules to be effective, it is important that the field for which you are setting the rule be formatted appropriately for the data type that should be entered. For example, if you set a validation rule requiring a four-digit number, the data type for the field should be set to Number. If you are requiring dates that occur before a specific date, the data type for the field should be Date/Time.

Validation Text Messages

When you set a validation rule for a field, it is also a good idea to set validation text, which contains instructions or valid data values to help guide data entry. Access displays the text as a message each time an invalid value is entered in the field.

Setting Different Types of Validation Rules

Validation rules are used to examine data entered into tables and forms. You can set comparison rules. Samples of comparison rules you can set to determine if the value is within a valid range are shown in the following table.

VALIDATION RULES

Comparison	Validation Rule Example	Validation Text Example
Greater than	>100	Enter a value greater than 100.
Less than	<100	Enter a value less than 100.
Equal to	=1 Or =2	Enter a value of 1 or 2.
Date after a date	>#1/1/2017#	Enter a date after January 1, 2017.
Greater than or equal to	>=100	Enter a value of 100 or more.
Less than or equal to	<=100	Enter a value of 100 or less.
Like	Like "ID-0000"	Enter a 4-digit value starting with *ID-*.
Between	Between 1 And 8	Enter a value from 1 to 8.

The same wildcards used to enter input masks are used in validation rules. For example, the question mark is substituted for each character that is required, such as in *ID-????*. The asterisk (*) can substitute for a group of characters that may vary, such as in *ID-**.

DEVELOP YOUR SKILLS: A5-D10

In this exercise, you will set validation rules for data entered into fields in the Products table.

1. Display the **Products** table in **Design View**.
2. Click anywhere in the **Price** field and then click in the **Validation Rule** field property box.
3. Type **>=25** as the validation rule.
4. Click in the **Validation Text** box and type **All prices must be at least $25**.
5. Choose **File→Save** or click the **Save** button and choose **Yes** when the warning message appears notifying you that the date integrity rules have been changed.

Test the New Validation Rules

6. Switch to **Datasheet View**.

   Notice that all the ProdID entries begin with PROD- *because of the input mask you set earlier.*

7. Click in the **ProdID** field for the new, blank record and type **07SW**.
8. Tap [Tab], type **Switchboard Page** as the description, and tap [Tab] again to move to the Price field.

9. Type **20** in the Price field and tap ⌈Tab⌉.

   The warning message appears because of the validation rule you just set for the Price field. Notice the
   All prices must be at least $25 *validation message you set is displayed in the alert.*

10. Click **OK** to acknowledge the error message, type **30** for the price, and tap ⌈Tab⌉.

11. Close the Products table.

Setting Lookup Fields with the Lookup Wizard

All tables in a relational database are related in some way to each other, as well as to other objects in the database. Data from one table is often used in another table. A lookup field enables you to select a field value in one table by looking up values from another table; or you could select from a list of values entered by the database designer. The list of valid entries appears in a drop-down menu in the table accessing the values.

A lookup field displays a menu arrow at the
right end of the field during data entry.

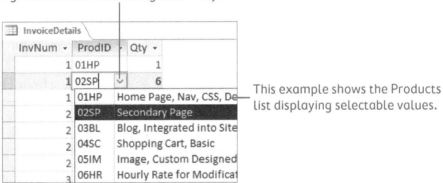

This example shows the Products
list displaying selectable values.

Using a lookup value also enables you to look up values from one field and return a value from a different field in the connected table. For example, you can look up a product number by typing the common product name.

Examining the Benefits of Lookup Tables

Adding a lookup field to a table serves three primary purposes:

▸ It reduces the time required to enter the data repeatedly.

▸ It reduces errors associated with data entry.

▸ It restricts data to valid entries.

For example, if you are processing time card data before issuing employee checks, setting a lookup field of valid employee IDs helps ensure that only valid employees receive checks. Lookup fields also help reduce the number of redundant fields contained in database tables.

Performing a Lookup

Access provides the following two ways to use the Lookup feature:

▶ **Lookup Wizard:** A data type that launches the Lookup Wizard, which walks you through the process of setting up a lookup field.

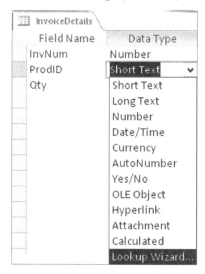

▶ **Lookup tab:** An option in the Design View Field Properties pane that sets the data source containing the values you want to display in the field.

DEVELOP YOUR SKILLS: A5-D11

In this exercise, you will delete the relationship between two tables and create a lookup field in the Products table that displays a list of valid products. You will then use the lookup field to enter data into the Invoice Details table.

1. Make sure the Products table is closed, as you cannot make relationship changes to an open table.
2. Choose **Database Tools→Relationships→Relationships** 🔳.
3. Right-click the **join line** linking the Products and InvoiceDetails tables.

   Your mouse pointer must be directly on the line for the desired menu to appear.
4. Choose **Delete** and then click **Yes** to confirm the deletion.
5. Using the same procedure, delete the relationship between the **EmpID** fields in the Employees and Invoices tables, and between **EmpID** in the Employees table and **EmployeeID** in the EmpSpouses table.
6. Close the Relationships window and save the changes.
7. Display the **InvoiceDetails** table in **Design View**.

8. Click in the **Data Type** box of the **ProdID** field and click the drop-down **menu** button ▼.

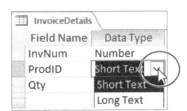

9. Choose **Lookup Wizard** from the menu.

10. Click **Next** to accept the current setting **I Want the Lookup Field to Get the Values from Another Table or Query**.

11. Choose **Table: Products** in the next Wizard screen, and then click **Next**.

   The Products table will contain the values to be looked up.

12. Move all three fields to the **Selected Fields** list and click **Next**.

13. Choose **ProdID** as the sort field, leave the sort order as **Ascending**, and click **Next**.

   The next Wizard screen lets you adjust the width of the lookup field columns, which determines how the columns appear when the lookup field is used.

14. Uncheck the **Hide Key Column** checkbox.

15. Double-click the right borders of all three column headings to Best Fit the columns and then click **Next**.

16. Click **Next** again to choose **ProdID** as the field that uniquely identifies the row.

17. In the next Wizard screen, check the **Enable Data Integrity** box and then choose the **Cascade Delete** option.

18. Click **Finish** and choose **Yes** in the warning box that appears.

19. Choose **Yes** again in the Some Data May Be Lost warning box.

Test the Lookup Field

20. Switch to **Datasheet View**.

21. Click in the **ProdID** field for the 02SP record (second record in the table).

22. Click the drop-down **menu** button ▼ and then choose the product **07SW**.

   This product ID replaces the 02SP for that record. So invoice 1 still has three products listed on it, but one of them has changed. This lookup field makes it easy for you to view a listing of products when adding them to invoices.

23. Close the InvoiceDetails table.

Creating Lookup Fields for Multiple Values

You have already created a lookup field that enabled you to select a single item from a list. You can also set up lists that allow you to select multiple values to enter for each lookup field. If, for example, an inventory item is available from more than one supplier, you can set up the field to allow you to select all suppliers for an item. To create a selection list, simply check the Multiple Items option as you move through the Lookup Wizard screens.

DEVELOP YOUR SKILLS: A5-D12

In this exercise, you will create a lookup field in the Invoices table that allows you to assign two or more employees to an inventory item.

1. Display the **Invoices** table in **Design View**

2. Click in the **Data Type** box of the **EmpID** field and click the **menu** button ▼.

3. Choose **Lookup Wizard** from the menu.

4. Click **Next** to accept the current setting, **I Want the Lookup Field to Get the Values from Another Table or Query**.

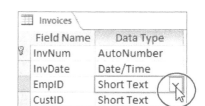

   If you choose the option I Will Type the Values in That I Want, *you can create your own list of items.*

5. Choose **Table: Employees** and click **Next**.

   The Employees table will contain the values to be looked up.

6. Move the **EmpID**, **EmpLastName**, and **EmpFirstName** fields to the Selected Fields list and click **Next**.

7. Choose **EmpID** as the sort field, leave the sort order as **Ascending**, and click **Next**.

8. Click **Next** to accept the default width settings for the columns.

9. In the final Wizard screen, check the **Allow Multiple Values** box, leave the label set to **EmpID**, and click **Finish**.

10. Choose **Yes** in the message box to confirm that you want to store multiple values.

11. Choose **Yes** again to save the table and choose **Yes** one last time to confirm the Some Data May Be Lost message.

Test the Multiple Values Lookup Field

12. Switch to **Datasheet View**.

13. Click in the **Emp ID** field for the **3rd record** (invoice 3).

14. Click the **drop-down menu** button ▼ to display the list of employees.

15. Check the boxes for **Winchester** and **Mansfield** and click **OK**.

16. Double-click the border between the Emp ID and Cust ID columns to Best Fit the Emp ID column.

   Invoice 3 now has two employees assigned to it. Notice both employee names are visible in the Emp ID field.

17. Choose **File→Close** to close the database and save the changes to the Invoices table.

Self-Assessment

Check your knowledge of this chapter's key concepts and skills using the Self-Assessment in your ebook or eLab course.

⚓ Reinforce Your Skills

Create and Edit Relationships; Modify Table Structure and Appearance

The president of Kids for Change, an organization that encourages young people to participate in community-based projects, has asked you to modify the K4C database. In this exercise, you will create a relationship between tables and create a relationship report. You will rename a table and add a new field, delete and modify fields, and enhance the datasheet with color.

1. Open **A5-R1-K4C** from your **Access Chapter 5** folder and save it as **A5-R1-K4CRevised**.

Create and Modify Table Relationships

2. Choose **Database Tools→Relationships→Relationships** ⊞.
3. Click the **Show Table** ⊞ button.
4. Add the **Volunteers** table to the Relationships window and then close the Show Table box.
5. Drag down the lower edge of the Volunteers field list to show all fields.
6. Drag the **ActID** field from the Activities table and drop it on the **ActID** field in the Volunteers table.
7. Check the **Enforce Referential Integrity** checkbox and click **Create** to establish the relationship.

    The join line has a 1 at the Activities table end and an infinity symbol, ∞, at the Volunteers table end.
8. Choose **Design→Tools→Relationship Report** ⊞.
9. Close the report, saving it as **Relationships**.
10. Close the **Relationships** window, saving the changes if prompted.

Modify the Table Structure

11. Right-click the **Staff** table and choose **Rename**.
12. Type **PaidStaff** and tap ⏎ Enter .
13. Display the **PaidStaff** table in **Design View**.
14. Right-click the row selector for the StaffStreet field and choose **Insert Rows**.
15. Click in the new **Field Name** box, type **Parent**, and tap ⏎ Tab .
16. Set the Data Type of the new field to **Yes/No**.
17. Enter **Parent of K4C child** in the Description box.
18. Switch to **Datasheet View** and save the table.
19. Check the Parent **Yes/No** boxes for parents with the last names of **Lockwood**, **Kendall**, and **Riggs**.
20. Close the PaidStaff table.
21. Open the **Donations** table in **Design View**.
22. Click the row selector for the Acknowledgement field and tap ⏎ Delete .
23. Choose **Yes** to confirm the deletion and then close the Donations table, saving the changes.

Format a Table Datasheet Layout

24. Display the **Children** table in **Datasheet View**.

25. Click on the **First Name** column heading and then hover the mouse pointer over the heading until the white pointer appears.

26. Drag the **First Name** column to the left of the Last Name column.

27. Drag the mouse pointer over the **Address**, **City**, **ST**, and **ZIP** columns to select those columns.

28. Right-click one of the selected column headings and choose **Hide Fields**.

29. Double-click the right edges of the Mother and Father column headings to Best Fit those columns.

30. Choose **Home→Text Formatting→Alternate Row Color** 🔲 **menu button** ▼ and choose any light alternate row color.

31. Choose **Home→Text Formatting→Gridlines** 🔲 **menu button** ▼ and choose **Gridlines: Horizontal**.

32. Choose **Home→Text Formatting** group dialog box launcher as shown below to open the Datasheet Formatting dialog box.

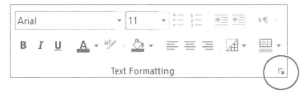

33. Choose the following settings in the Datasheet Formatting box:
- Choose a dark Gridline Color to create a nice contrast with the light alternate row color you chose.
- In the Border and Line Styles section, choose **Column Header Underline** as the border style.
- In the Border and Line Styles section, choose **Dots** as the line style.

34. Click **OK** to apply the formats to the datasheet.

35. Choose **File→Close** to close the database, saving the changes to the Children table.

REINFORCE YOUR SKILLS: A5-R2

Set Field Properties, Apply Input Masks, and Create Lookup Fields

As head of Tech Development for Kids for Change, you want to set some database field properties. In this exercise, you will set field size, convert values to uppercase, set captions and default values, make a field required, and create a custom format for an ID field. You will set a predefined telephone input mask, add a validation rule, and set a lookup field.

1. Open **A5-R2-K4C** from your **Access Chapter 5** folder and save it as **A5-R2-K4CRevised**.

Set Table Field Properties

2. Display the **Volunteers** table in **Design View**.

3. Set the Field Size property of the VolID field to **12**.

4. Set the Field Size property of the VolLastName field to **25** and use **Last Name** as the Caption.

ACCESS

5. Set the Field Size property of the VolFirstName field to **25** and use **First Name** as the Caption.

6. Set the Field Size property of the VolStreet field to **25** and use **Street** as the Caption.

7. Set the Field Size property of the VolCity field to **25** and use **City** as the Caption.

8. Set the following properties for the VolST field:

   Field Size: **2**
   Format: **>**
   Caption: **ST**
   Default Value: **FL**

   Using > as the Format property will convert lowercase values to uppercase values.

9. Set the Field Size property of the VolZIP field to **5** and use **ZIP Code** as the Caption.

10. Set the Field Size property of the VolPhone field to **15** and use **Telephone** as the Caption.

11. Set the Field Size property of the ActID field to **6** and use **Act/Day** as the Caption.

12. Set the Required property of the ActID field to **Yes**.

13. Switch to **Datasheet View** and choose **Yes** to save the table, then choose **Yes** again when the Some Data May Be Lost message appears, and choose **Yes** a third time when the data integrity message appears.

14. Enter the following new record into the table:

Field Name	Value
VolID	**10**
LastName	**Graves**
FirstName	**Matthew**
Street	**915 Beneva St**
City	**Sarasota**
ST	**FL**
ZIPCode	**34232**
Telephone	**9415556198**
Act/Day	**BCSat**

15. Close the Volunteers table.

Set an Input Mask and Validation Rules

16. Display the **Activities** table in **Design View**.

17. Set the Input Mask property of the ActID field to **"K4C-">LLL<LL**.

    This input mask starts each ActID with the literal value K4C- followed by three uppercase (>) letters and two lowercase (<) letters; for example, K4C-DWTue for dog walking on Tuesday.

18. Switch to **Datasheet View**, saving the changes to the table.

19. Scroll to the end of the table and click in the first empty **Activity ID** field.

    Access automatically places the new prefix in the field because of the input mask you just created.

20. Close the Activities table.

21. Display the **Volunteers** table in **Datasheet View**.

    Notice the Telephone field displays numbers with no formatting.

22. Switch to **Design View**.

23. Click anywhere in the **VolPhone** field and then click in the **Input Mask** property box.

24. Click the **Build** ⋯ button to start the Input Mask Wizard.

25. Choose the **Phone Number** mask and click **Finish**.

26. Switch to **Datasheet View**, saving the changes to the table.

    Notice the Telephone field is now formatted with the input mask characters.

27. Close the Volunteers table.

28. Display the **Children** table in **Design View**.

29. Set the Validation Rule property of the BirthDate field to **>01/01/2002**.

30. Enter **Only children born after January 1, 2002, may enroll** in the Validation Text property.

31. Switch to **Datasheet View**, choose **Yes** to save the table, and then choose **Yes** again when the data integrity message appears.

32. Enter the following information into a new record:

Field Name	Value
ChildID	CasadoM
LastName	Casado
FirstName	Marty
Address	302 Waterside Ave
City	Bradenton
ST	FL
ZIP	34202
Telephone	9415551652
BirthDate	11/24/2001

    The input mask will not allow you to enter the birth date since it is prior to 01/01/2002.

33. Click **OK** and then change the Birth Date value to **11/24/2002**.

34. Complete the record by entering **Sandy** for Mother, **Javier** for Father, and **9415551653** for Emergency.

Set a Field as a Lookup Field

35. Switch to **Design View**.

36. Click anywhere in the **ChildST** field and then click the **Lookup** tab in the Field Properties box and choose **Combo Box** as the Display Control as shown here.

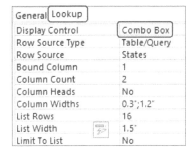

37. Enter the following Lookup properties, which are also shown in the image above:

Row Source: **States**
Column Count: **2**
Column Widths: **0.3", 1.2"**
List Width: **1.5"**

38. Switch to **Datasheet View** and save the changes to the table.

39. Click in the **ST** field for *DriverJ*, which is missing the state.

40. Open the combo box of lookup values and choose **FL**.

41. Choose **File→Close** to close the database, saving the changes to the Children table.

REINFORCE YOUR SKILLS: A5-R3

Set Relationships, Format Datasheets, Set Field Properties, and Add a Lookup Field

The Kids for Change database is performing better, but you want to modify database tables to improve their appearance and facilitate data entry and validation. In this exercise, you will add a field to indicate whether a staffer has a master's degree, delete a table that K4C no longer uses, and rearrange fields. You will also hide a field for confidentiality reasons, resize columns to better display data, create a custom input mask with data validation that requires certain categories of donations, and apply a predefined input mask using the Wizard.

1. Open **A5-R3-K4C** from your **Access Chapter 5** folder and save it as **A5-R3-K4CRevised**.

Create and Edit Relationships

2. Choose **Database Tools→Relationships→Relationships** ⊞.

3. Establish a relationship by dragging the **DonorID** field from the Donors table to the **DonorID** field in the Donations table.

4. Check the **Enforce Referential Integrity** checkbox and click **Create**.

5. Choose **Design→Tools→Relationship Report** ⊞.

6. Close the report, saving it as **Relationships**, and then close the Relationships window.

Modify the Table Structure

7. Display the **PaidStaff** table in **Design View**.

8. Right-click the **ActID** row selector and choose **Insert Rows**.

9. Type **Masters** for the new field name.

10. Set the Data Type to **Yes/No** and enter **Master's Degree or higher** as the Description.

11. Switch to **Datasheet View** and save the table.

12. Check the **Master's** checkboxes for records with the last names of **Bryant**, **Lockwood**, and **Riggs**.

13. Switch to **Design View**.

14. Click the **field selector** box for the **2ndDay** field and tap Delete to remove the field.

15. Choose **Yes** to confirm the deletion.

16. Switch to **Datasheet View** and save the table.

Format a Table Datasheet Layout

17. Move the **Email Address** column to the left of the Master's column.

18. If necessary, scroll to the right until the HrlySal column is visible.

19. Right-click the **HrlySal** column heading and choose **Hide Fields**.

    The hourly salary field is no longer displayed, but the data remains in the table.

20. If necessary, scroll to the left and then double-click the right edge of the **Email Address** column heading to Best Fit the column.

    All email addresses should now be visible.

21. Choose **Home→Text Formatting→Alternate Row Color** ⊞ **menu button** ▼ and choose any light alternate row color.

22. Choose **Home→Text Formatting→Gridlines** ⊞ **menu button** ▼ and choose **Gridlines: Horizontal**.

23. Click the **dialog box launcher** at the bottom-right corner of the Text Formatting group to open the Datasheet Formatting dialog box.

24. Open the **Gridline Color** menu, choose a dark color to complement the light row color, and then click **OK**.

25. Close the **PaidStaff** table, saving the changes.

Set Field Properties

26. Display the **Donors** table in **Design View**.

27. Set the following field sizes and captions:

Field Name	Field Size	Caption
DonorLName	25	Last Name
DonorFName	25	First Name
DonorStreet	25	Street
DonorCity	25	City
DonorST	2	ST
DonorZIP	5	ZIP
DonorPhone	15	Telephone
DonorEmail	No Change	Email Address

28. Set the Required property of the DonorLName field to **Yes** and set the Allow Zero Length property to **No**.

29. Set the Format property of the DonorST field to **>** and set the Default Value property to **FL**.

30. Switch to **Datasheet View**, saving the changes to the table, choosing **Yes** in the warning box, and choosing **Yes** again in the second warning box.

31. Enter the following record into the table:

Field Name	Value
DonorID	Automatically set
LastName	**Castro**
FirstName	**Lana**
Street	**4040 Conquistador Way**
City	**Bradenton**
ST	**FL**
ZIP	**34212**
Telephone	**9415556626**
EmailAddress	**MCastro@email.com**
Acknowledgement	**For Mina**

32. Close the Donors table when you have finished.

Set Formats, Input Masks, and Allow Zero Length

33. Display the **Donations** table in **Design View**.

34. Set the following field properties in the DonationType field:

Input Mask: **>L<LL**
Validation Rule: **Bus Or Pvt**
Validation Text: **Must be Bus or Pvt**

35. Switch to **Datasheet View**, saving the changes to the table and choosing **Yes** in both warning boxes.

36. Add this record to test the new input mask:

Field Name	Value
DonorID	**12**
DonationDate	**04152013**
Amount	**1000**
DonationType	**Pmt**

37. Tap ⌗Tab⌗ after entering the donation type.

The validation text message appears because Pmt is not an allowable DonationType entry. This is because the validation rule you set only allows entries of Bus or Pvt.

38. Click **OK** and then type **Pvt** in the DonationType field.

39. Close the Donations table.

40. Display the **Donors** table in **Design View**.

41. Set the Format property of the Acknowledgement field to **@; No Comments**.

This will display the phrase No Comments *when the acknowledgement field is left blank.*

42. Click anywhere in the **DonorPhone** field and then click in the **Input Mask** property box.

43. Click the **Build** ⋯ button to start the Input Mask Wizard.

44. Save the table when prompted.

45. Choose the **Phone Number** mask and click **Finish**.

46. Switch to **Datasheet View**, saving the changes to the table.

Notice that all telephone numbers now have proper and consistent formatting. Also notice that the phrase No Comments *appears in all records where no Acknowledgement was entered.*

47. Close the Donors table.

Set a Field as a Lookup Field

48. Display the **PaidStaff** table in **Design View**.

49. Click anywhere in the **ActID** field and then click the Lookup tab in the Field Properties box and choose **Combo Box** as the Display Control.

50. Enter the following Lookup properties:

Row Source: `Activities`
Column Count: `2`
Column Widths: `0.5"; 1.5"`
List Width: `2"`

51. Switch to **Datasheet View** and save the changes to the table.

52. Right-click the **Email Address** column heading and choose **Unhide Fields**.

53. Check the **HrlySal** box and then close the Unhide Columns box.

The hourly salary field, which had been hidden, reappears.

54. Test the new lookup field by adding this record:

Field Name	Value
StaffID	Automatically entered
LastName	**Francesco**
FirstName	**Dominic**
Parent	**Yes** (checked)
StreetAddress	**105 26th Street**
City	**Sarasota**
ST	**FL**
ZIP	**34209**
Telephone	**9415558287**
Masters	Yes (checked)

55. Type **E** in the Activity field.

Access displays the first value that begins with the letter E: EBSun.

56. Tap Tab to accept the EBSun entry.

57. Type **27** in the Hrly Sal field and **DomFrancesco@email.com** in the Email Address field.

58. Choose **File→Close** to close the database, saving changes to any tables if prompted to do so.

 Apply Your Skills

Create and Edit Relationships; Modify Table Structure and Appearance

The CEO of Universal Corporate Events, Ltd., has asked you to make some changes to the UCE database. In this exercise, you will create a relationship between two tables, set referential integrity, and create a relationship report. Then you will rename and add a Yes/No field to a table, and delete, modify, and rearrange fields. Finally, you will improve the appearance of the Menus table.

1. Open **A5-A1-UCE** from your **Access Chapter 5** folder and save it as **A5-A1-UCERevised**.

Add, Delete, Modify, and Print Table Relationships

2. Establish a relationship between the VenueID fields in the Venues and Schedules tables enforcing referential integrity.

3. Create a Relationships Report named **Relationships**.

4. Close the report and the Relationships window.

Modify a Table's Structure and Column Display

5. Change the name of the Contacts table to **VenueLiaisons**.

6. Insert a new field in the Venues table above the VenueWebSite field and use the following settings:

   Field Name: **Kitchen**
   Data Type: **Yes/No**
   Description: **Does venue have a kitchen?**

7. Switch to **Datasheet View**, saving the changes, and check the **Yes/No** Kitchen boxes for **HyattS**, **ManYC**, and **SaraCC**, **SaraYC**, and **TmpCon**.

8. Close the Venues table when you have finished.

9. Open the **Schedules** table in **Design View**.

10. Delete the VenueName field and then close the Schedules table, saving the changes.

11. Display the **Personnel** table in **Datasheet View**.

12. Move the **Date Hired** field to the left of the Last Name column.

13. Hide the Date of Birth field so it is no longer displayed.

14. Apply Best Fit to the Address and Email Address columns to make the widest entries in the columns fully visible.

15. Close the Personnel table, saving the changes.

Change the Formatting of a Datasheet

16. Display the **Menus** table in **Datasheet View**.

17. Apply a light Alternate Row Color.

18. Apply Horizontal Gridlines and change the Gridline Color to black.

19. Close the database, saving the changes to the Menus table.

Set Field Properties, Apply Input Masks, and Create Lookup Fields

UCE has asked for your help again. In this exercise, you will modify field properties in the UCE database tables to more accurately describe and limit the data. You will set field sizes and captions, convert field values to uppercase, set a default value for easier data entry, and make a field required. You will also set a custom format for an ID field, apply a predefined input mask to a telephone field, add a validation rule so that no event with less than 35 guests can be entered, and you will finish by setting lookup fields.

1. Open **A5-A2-UCE** from your **Access Chapter 5** folder and save it as **A5-A2-UCERevised**.

Set Field Properties

2. Display the **VenueLiaisons** table in **Design View** and set the following field sizes and captions:

Field Name	Field Size	Caption
LiaisonID	12	
LiaisonLName	25	Last Name
LiaisonFName	25	First Name
LiaisonStreet	25	Street
LiaisonCity	25	City
LiaisonState	2	State
LiaisonZIP	5	ZIP Code
LiaisonPhone	15	Telephone
LiaisonEmail		Email Address

3. Set the Required property of the LiaisonPhone field to **Yes** and set the Allow Zero Length property to **No**.

4. Set the Default Value property of the LiaisonState field to **FL**.

5. Switch to **Datasheet View**, saving the changes to the table and choosing **Yes** in the warning boxes, and then add the following record:

Field Name	Value
LiaisonID	AntonV
LastName	Anton
FirstName	Vera
Street	44 West Florida St.
City	Bradenton
State	FL
ZIP	34205
Telephone	9415554248
EmailAddress	VAnton@email.com

6. Close the VenueLiaisons table when you have finished.

Create a Custom Field Format, Set an Input Mask and Validation Rules, and Set a Field as a Lookup Field

7. Display the **Personnel** table in **Design View**.

8. Set the following properties for the PerID field:

   Field Size: **10**
   Input Mask: **"UCE-"9999**
   Caption: **ID**

   Each PerID will start with the literal value UCE, followed by four numbers, such as UCE-1001.

9. Switch to **Datasheet View**, saving the changes to the table and responding **Yes** to the warning message.

10. Click in the empty **ID** field in the new record at the bottom of the table.

    If your input mask is set up properly, Access will automatically add the prefix UCE to the entry.

11. Close the Personnel table once you have verified that your input mask is set up properly.

12. Display the **VenueLiaisons** table in **Design View**.

13. Use the Input Mask Wizard to apply the **Phone Number** mask to the LiaisonPhone field.

14. Switch to **Datasheet View**, saving the changes to the VenueLiaisons table.

    The telephone numbers should now have the input mask applied.

15. Close the VenueLiaisons table.

16. Display the **Schedules** table in **Design View**.

17. Set the following field properties for the Guests field:

    Validation Rule: **>=35**
    Validation Text: **At least 35 guests must be entered**

18. Click anywhere in the **EventID** field and then click the **Lookup** tab in the Field Properties box and choose **Combo Box** as the Display Control.

19. Set the following Lookup properties:

    Row Source: **Events**
    Column Count: **2**
    Column Widths: **0.6"; 1.5"**
    List Width: **2.1"**

20. Click anywhere in the **Menu Code** field and then click the **Lookup** tab in the Field Properties box and choose **Combo Box** as the Display Control.

21. Set the following Lookup properties:

    Row Source: **Menus**
    Column Count: **2**
    Column Widths: **0.6" 1.5"**
    List Width: **2.1"**

22. Switch to **Datasheet View** and save the changes to the table, responding **Yes** to any warning messages.

23. Enter the following record:

Field Name	Value
ScheduleID	**SEMBenson**
VenueID	**ManCtr**
EventID	**SEMNAR**
MenuCode	**DINBUF**
EventDate	7/3/2017
Guests	30

Notice Access displays a validation text message since the number of guests entered is less than the minimum of 35.

24. Click **OK**, change the number of **Guests** to **40**, and add **Miller** in the Liaison field.

25. Close the database, saving the changes to the table if prompted.

APPLY YOUR SKILLS: A5-A3

Set Relationships, Format Datasheets, Set Field Properties, and Add a Lookup Field

The CEO of Universal Corporate Events, Ltd., wants you to clean up the appearance of the company's database tables and improve data readability and validation. In this exercise, you will add a new field to indicate salaried positions, delete a field UCE no longer uses, and rearrange fields. You will also hide the cost per person in the Menus table, resize columns and set field sizes, and modify a field to convert data to uppercase. Finally, you will set captions, default values, and field requirements, create a custom input mask, and modify a field to look up values.

1. Open **A5-A3-UCE** from your **Access Chapter 5** folder and save it as **A5-A3-UCERevised**.

2. Establish a relationship by dragging the **Grade** field in the SalaryGrades table to the **SalaryGrade** field in the Personnel table, enforcing referential integrity.

3. Create a Relationships Report named **Relationships**.

4. Review the Object Dependencies and close the Object Dependencies panel when you have finished.

Modify Table Structure and Column Display

5. Display the **SalaryGrades** table in **Design View**.

6. Insert a new field in the SalaryGrades table above the Salary field using the following settings:
Field Name: **Salaried**
Data Type: **Yes/No**
Description: **Indicates salaried position**

7. Switch to **Datasheet View**, saving the changes, and check the **Yes/No** boxes for each record that has data in the Salary field.

8. Close the SalaryGrades table when you have finished.

9. Display the **Events** table in **Design View**.

10. Delete the **MinGuests** field and then close the Events table, saving the changes.

11. Display the **VenueLiaisons** table in **Datasheet View**.

12. Select both the **Telephone** and **Email Address** columns and move them to the left of the Street Address column.

13. Apply Best Fit to all the columns and then close the table, saving the changes.

14. Display the **Menus** table in **Datasheet View**.

15. Hide the Cost/PP field and then close the table, saving the changes.

Change the Formatting of a Datasheet and Set Field Properties

16. Display the **Venues** table in **Datasheet View**.

17. Apply a light Alternate Row Color.

18. Apply Horizontal Gridlines and change the Gridline Color to black.

19. Close the Venues table, saving the changes.

Set Captions, Default Values, and Field Requirements

20. Display the **Personnel** table in **Design View** and set the following field sizes and captions:

Field Name	Field Size	Caption
PerLastName	25	Last Name
PerFirstName	25	First Name
PerAddr	25	Street
PerCity	25	City
PerST	2	State
PerZIP	5	ZIP Code
PerPhone	15	Telephone
SalaryGrade		Salary Grade

21. Set the Required property of the PerLastName field to **Yes**.

22. Set the Default Value property of the PerST field to **FL**.

23. Close the table, saving the changes and choosing **Yes** in the warning boxes.

Set Formats, Input Masks, Allow Zero Length, and Lookup Fields

24. Display the **Schedules** table in **Design View**.

25. Enter **>LLLL<??????** as the Input Mask field property for the ScheduleID field.

    This mask forces 4 uppercase letters followed by from 0 to 6 lowercase letters.

26. Switch to **Datasheet View**, saving the changes.

27. Scroll down and type a series of 10 lowercase letters in the ScheduleID field of a new record.

    Because of the input mask, Access converts the first 4 letters to uppercase.

28. Tap Esc to remove the data you just entered.

29. Type a series of 8 uppercase letters in the ScheduleID field.

    Because of the input mask, Access converts all but the first 4 letters to lowercase.

30. Tap ⎡Esc⎤ to exit the record without saving.

31. Close the Schedules table, choosing **OK** and **Yes** when prompted.

32. Display the **Venues** table in **Design View**.

33. Set the Format field property of the VenueWebSite field to **@; No Website**

This will display No Website if there is no data in the VenueWebSite field.

34. Set the Allow Zero Length property of the VenueLiaison field to **No**.

35. Choose **File→Save** or click the **Save** button and save the **Venues** table, choosing **Yes** in the warning box.

36. Use the Input Mask Wizard to apply the Phone Number mask to the VenuePhone field.

37. Click anywhere in the **VenueST** field and then click the **Lookup** tab in the Field Properties box and choose **Combo Box** as the Display Control.

38. Set the following Lookup properties:

Row Source: **States**
Column Count: **2**
Column Widths: **0.3"; 1.2"**
List Width: **1.5"**

39. Switch to **Datasheet View**, saving the changes if prompted, and enter the following record:

Field Name	Value
VenueID	**BradCC**
Name	**Bradenton Country Club**
Street	**2903 9th Ave**
City	**Bradenton**
ST	**FL**
ZIP	**34205**
Phone	**9415550031**
Kitchen	**Yes**
Website	**bcc.com**
Liaison	**AntonV**

40. Close the database, saving the changes to the Venues table and any other open tables.

 Extend Your Skills

These exercises challenge you to think critically and apply your new skills. You will be evaluated on your ability to follow directions, completeness, creativity, and the use of proper grammar and mechanics. Save files to your chapter folder. Submit assignments as directed.

A5-E1 That's the Way I See It

You've been asked to enhance the table structure in the Blue Jean Landscaping database. Open **A5-E1-BJL** and save it as **A5-E1-BJLRevised**. Create a relationship between the MerchID fields in the StoreMerchandise and SalesInvoices tables, enforcing referential integrity, and creating a relationships report named **BJL Relationships**. Autofit all columns in the StoreMerchandise table, apply the input mask "BJL"-9999 to the MerchID field, and switch the order of the Manufacturer and ItemName fields. In the Customers table, make the last name required, display the message *No Email* for customers without an email address, and use the Input Mask Wizard to apply the Phone Number input mask to the CustTelephone field.

A5-E2 Be Your Own Boss

As the owner of Blue Jean Landscaping, you want to improve how your database looks and behaves. Open **A5-E2-BJL** and save it as **A5-E2-BJLRevised**. Create relationships between the CustID fields in the Customers and SalesInvoices tables and between the CustID fields in the Customers and ServiceInvoices tables, enforcing referential integrity, and creating a relationships report named **BJL Relationships**. In the ServiceInvoices table, hide the ServID field, autofit all remaining columns, and make all fields required. In the ServiceReps table, apply the input mask "BJLRep-"9999 to the RepID field and the Phone Number input mask to the RepPhone field. Finally, set RepState as a combo box lookup field with the field properties Row Source=States, Column Count=2, Column Widths=0.5", 1.5", List Width=2".

A5-E3 Demonstrate Proficiency

Stormy BBQ is continuing to update its database as it remodels its flagship location in Key West to give it a more tropical look and feel. (It has also added more employees.) Open **A5-E3-SBQ** and save it as **A5-E3-SBQRevised**. Apply the techniques you learned in this chapter to format and dress up the Staff table. Be sure to set appropriate field sizes and captions, autofit columns as needed, and display the text *No Email Available* for staff members who don't have an email address.

6

Customizing Input Forms

In this chapter, you will learn how to add a subform to a main form, which is a handy technique used to include data from a different source. You will also explore additional Access features to create calculated fields, add helpful tips to form controls, and set control properties to protect and limit data entry.

LEARNING OBJECTIVES

- Create a form that contains a subform
- Add a calculated control to a form
- Add a total row to a form
- Disable form fields
- Lock form fields
- Add screen tips to forms
- Create pop-up forms

📂 Project: Formatting Functional Forms

Winchester Web Design has seen sales increase over recent months and wants to simplify data entry. You must design advanced forms to make data entry easier and less prone to errors. You will create an Invoice form that contains a subform containing invoice details. Your form will also contain a calculated field for creating totals, and you will use form features to enhance data entry. The database relationships will be critical for setting up these forms.

Subforms

Although many forms are designed to enter data into a single table, there are times when you may need forms that perform actions such as processing customer invoices, calculating totals, and locating data from multiple tables. One of the best ways to accomplish this is through a subform, which is a secondary form placed on the main form. Subforms work well when one-to-many relationships are set, allowing the user to use multiple tables on a single form. Subforms are simply subsets of data linked by parent fields on the main form to child fields on the subform.

Main form displaying customer and employee information

Detail data from related tables appears in a subform.

Creating Subforms

The easiest way to create a subform is with the Form Wizard, which contains an option to add a subform. Subforms can be added to existing forms using the Subform control in the Property Sheet. When this option is used, you are able to specify the position and size of the subform on the main form. A Subform Wizard is then launched, in which you specify the subform properties.

≡ Create→Forms→Form Wizard 🖾; Design→Controls→Subform 🖼

DEVELOP YOUR SKILLS: A6-D1

In this exercise, you will use the Form Wizard to create an invoice form that contains an invoice details subform.

1. Open **A6-D1-WinWebDesign** from your **Access Chapter 6** folder and save it as **A6-D1-WinWebDesignRevised**.

2. Click the **Invoices** table in the Navigation pane.

3. Choose **Create→Forms→Form Wizard** 📑.

4. Add **InvNum** and **CustID** to the Selected Fields list.

5. Choose **Table: Customers** from the Tables/Queries list then add the following fields to the Selected Fields list: **CustLastName**, **CustFirstName**, **CustStreetAddress**, **CustCity**, **CustState**, **CustZIP**, **CustPhone**, and **CustEmail**.

6. Add the fields from the following tables to the Selected Fields list in the order shown here:

   It's important that you add the fields in the order shown.

Table	Fields
Invoices	InvDate
Employees	EmpID
	EmpLastName
	EmpFirstName
InvoiceDetails	ProdID
Products	ProdDescription
	Price
InvoiceDetails	Qty

7. Click **Next** and notice the data is arranged by Invoices and the **Form with Subform(s)** option is already chosen.

   Notice the subform preview shown in the Wizard contains the ProdID, ProdDescription, Price, and Qty fields.

8. Click **Next** to accept the settings and then click **Next** again to accept the Datasheet layout for the subform.

9. In the final Wizard screen, name the form **Customer Invoices**, name the subform **Customer InvoiceDetails Subform**, and click **Finish**.

   The new form and subform display in Form View.

10. Double-click the right border of each subform column heading to autofit the columns.

11. Click in the empty **ProdID** cell in the new row at the bottom of the subform.

12. Click the drop-down **menu** button ▼ and choose **03BL**.

    Notice how easy it was to populate the first three fields of the new subform record.

13. Enter **1** in the Qty column and tap Tab to complete the record.

Modifying Subforms

When a subform is created with the Form Wizard, Access creates both the subform and a main form with the subform embedded within it, and it displays both in the Navigation pane. The subform can then be opened and modified by itself in either Layout View or Design View. Or the main form can be opened and both it and the embedded subform can be modified together.

The Customer InvoiceDetails Subform and the Customer Invoices main form are displayed in the Navigation pane.

Subforms and their controls have their own Property Sheets that allow you to precisely control the subform layout and design. And you can use the same keystroke and mouse techniques to arrange and size subform controls that you use with main forms.

DEVELOP YOUR SKILLS: A6-D2

In this exercise, you will modify the Customer Invoices form and subform by deleting, moving, and sizing controls, and adding a graphic to the form.

1. Switch to **Layout View**.

Layout and Size Controls on the Main Form

2. Click the **ST** label in the main form to select it and then click inside the label and change it to **State**.

3. Change the *ZIP* label to **Zip**.

4. Locate the *EmpID* label and notice the *Last Name* and *First Name* labels below it.

5. Change the employee *Last Name* label to **Emp Last Name** and the employee *First Name* label to **Emp First Name**.

6. Display the Property Sheet by choosing **Design→Tools→Property Sheet** 📋.

    As you select and move controls in the following steps, you may need to drag the Property Sheet out of the way or close and reopen it as needed.

7. Select the text boxes shown here by pressing and holding the Ctrl key while clicking the boxes, and then set the Width property to **1"**.

8. Select the text boxes shown here and set the Width property to **2"**.

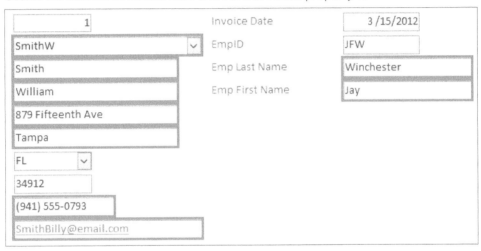

Layout and Size Controls on the Subform

9. Select the *CustomerInvoiceDetails* label on the subform and tap Delete to remove it.

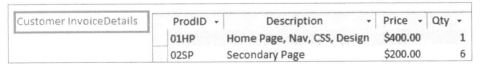

10. Click the right border of the subform frame and then drag left until the frame is slightly wider than the subform.

11. With the subform frame still selected, use the left arrow ⬅ key to nudge the subform to the left until it aligns with the main form labels.

Modify the Form Header

In the next few steps, you will modify the form title and add color and a logo to the header.

12. Use these guidelines to modify the form as shown here:
- Click just in front of *Invoices* in the title box and then press Shift + Enter to move *Invoices* to a new line.
- Click on the right border of the title box and then drag right to widen the box by about **0.5"**.
- Replace *Customer* with **Winchester Web Design**
- Adjust the box width again so it is just wide enough to keep *Winchester Web Design* on a single line.
- Select both lines and use **Home→Text Formatting→Center** ≡ to center the title within the box.

13. Click to the right of the title box in an empty part of the Form Header.

The title box will become deselected and the Form Header will become selected.

14. If necessary, display the Property Sheet and click in the **Back Color** property box.

15. Click the **Build** ⋯ button and choose a light blue color or whatever color you feel looks best in the Form Header.

16. Choose **Design→Header/Footer→Logo** 🖼.

17. Navigate to your **Access Chapter 6** folder, choose **WWD-Logo.jpg**, and click **OK**.

18. Set the Width and Height properties to **0.8"** and the Left property to **4"**.

19. Review your completed form and then close it, saving the changes to both the form and subform.

Adding Calculations to Forms

There are several ways to add calculations to forms. The easiest way is to build a form based on a query that already has a calculated field. If your form is based on one or more tables or is based on a query without a calculated field, then other methods are used.

Applying Totals to Forms in Datasheet Layout

The Form Wizard has an option that lets you create a form in Datasheet Layout View. A form in Datasheet Layout View looks just like a table in Datasheet View. The Totals feature is available for tables in Datasheet View and for forms in Datasheet Layout View. The Totals feature lets you easily use aggregate functions such as count, sum, and average to create totals for numeric fields in the datasheet.

☰ Home → Records→Totals $\boxed{\Sigma}$

DEVELOP YOUR SKILLS: A6-D3

In this exercise, you will create a form that uses the Totals feature to count the number of individual line items on customer invoices and to total the amounts of all invoices.

1. Choose **Invoices Query** in the Navigation pane and then choose **Create→Forms→Form Wizard** .

2. Move all fields to the Selected Fields list and then click **Next**.

3. Choose **Datasheet** as the layout and click **Next**.

4. Name the new form **Invoices Query Form** and click **Finish**.

   Notice the form looks like a table displayed in Datasheet View.

5. **Choose Home→Records→Totals** **Σ**.

   Notice a Total line appears at the bottom of the datasheet layout.

10	7/30/2012 Secondary Page
11	8/15/2012 Secondary Page
Total	

   Record: |◄ ◄ 1 of 125 ► ►| ►⁘   No Filter   Search

6. Click in the **Qty** cell on the Total row and choose **Count,** and then click in the **LineTotal** cell and choose **Sum**.

   The Count function simply counts the number of rows containing a Qty while the Sum function adds all LineTotals in the column.

10	7/30/2012 Secondary Page	$200.00	1	$200.00
11	8/15/2012 Secondary Page	$200.00	5	$1,000.00
Total			**125**	**$62,920.00**

   Record: |◄ ◄ 1 of 125 ► ►| ►⁘   No Filter   Search

7. Scroll down through the datasheet's 125 rows and notice that the Total row remains fixed at the bottom of the window.

   The Totals feature is an easy way to use aggregate functions (count, sum, average) and is available in forms and in tables and queries.

8. Close the Invoices Query Form, saving the changes if prompted.

Creating Calculated Controls in Forms

The Totals feature is useful when you want to create totals for all records in a datasheet. But sometimes it is necessary to display calculations in Form View, which displays just a single record at a time. This is done by inserting a new text box control on the form and inserting a formula in the Control Source property. The formula references other controls on the form that are bound to underlying database fields. For example, you would use the formula =Price*Qty to display the total amount of a transaction, with both the Price and Qty shown on the form.

In this exercise, you will add a calculated control to the Customer InvoiceDetails subform.

1. Display the **Customer InvoiceDetails** subform in **Design View**.

Insert a New Control

2. Position the mouse pointer on the top edge of the **Form Footer** section bar until the resize pointer appears and then drag down slightly to make room for a new text box.

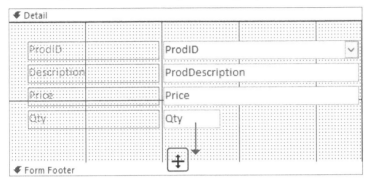

3. Choose **Design→Controls→Text Box** .

4. Click in the space you just created below the Qty control to insert a new control as shown here.

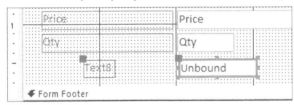

5. Use the arrow keys as needed to nudge the control so it is aligned with the Qty control.

   You will nudge the label, Text8, in a later step.

Create a Formula

6. Make sure the new control is still selected and, if necessary, choose **Design→Tools→Property Sheet** to display the Property Sheet.

7. Click the **All** tab in the Property Sheet box and set these four properties:

   Name: **Line Total**
   Control Source: **=Price*Qty**
   Format: **Currency**
   Decimal Places: **2**

Line Total	⌄
Format Data Event Other [All]	
Name	Line Total
Control Source	=Price*Qty
Format	Currency
Decimal Places	2
Visible	Yes

8. Click the *Text8* label on the subform and set the following properties:

Caption: **Invoice Total**
Width: **1"**
Left: **0.25"**

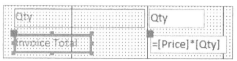

9. Switch to **Form View** to see your new calculated control in action.

10. Navigate to record 16 and other records where the Qty is greater than 1, and notice your calculated control always performs the correct calculations.

11. Close the form when you have finished and save the changes.

Setting Properties to Assist and Control Data Entry

Properties are available to assist with data entry, while others help control or limit it. These properties are easily set using the Property Sheet.

Disabling Form Fields

In some circumstances, a form may include data that users should not enter themselves or access. Many forms also contain settings that enter default values such as states or values such as cities that correspond to data contained in fields such as ZIP codes. To protect a field on a form from being edited or to allow a field to be skipped during data entry, you can disable the field in the Property Sheet. Disabled fields are unavailable for data entry. When a field is disabled, it is still visible but appears grayed out and is not accessible to the user. During data entry, Access skips disabled fields and moves directly to the next field that is enabled and accessible on a form. To disable a field, set the Enabled property to No.

Locking Form Fields

Another way to protect fields from being edited is by locking them. The advantage of locking a field is that it appears available on the form. The user can click in the field but cannot change the data. Many people prefer locking a field, rather than disabling it, because locked fields improve readability when a form is printed, whereas grayed, disabled fields print faintly. To lock a field, set the Locked property to Yes.

In this exercise, you will disable the InvNum field in the Customer Invoices form and the LineTotal field in the Customer InvoiceDetails subform. In addition, you will lock the Price field in the subform so that it cannot be edited.

1. Display the **Customer Invoices** form in **Design View**.
2. Click the **InvNum** text box on the main form and then click the **Data** tab on the Property Sheet.
3. Disable the text box by changing the Enabled property to **No**.
4. Click the **subform** and then disable the ProdID text box.
5. Click the **Price** text box in the subform and set the Locked property to **Yes**.

Test the Property Settings

6. Switch to **Form View** and try clicking in the disabled **InvNum** field.

   Notice the field is grayed out and you can't click in it.

7. Try clicking in any of the cells of the disabled ProdID field in the subform.

   In the subform, the field does not appear grayed out, but you still cannot click in it.

8. Click in any **Price** field in the subform and try changing the number.

   Locking allows a field to be entered, but the data cannot be changed.

Adding Control Tips

When you create a table and define fields, you have the opportunity to enter a description of the field in the Description column. These field descriptions appear in the status bar when the fields are active during data entry. These field descriptions also appear in the status bar when a field appears on a form. Although forms identify most fields with control labels, sometimes labels for specific fields such as State and ZIP are removed from a form when the controls are grouped together under a more general label such as *Address*. To help data entry personnel determine what data to type in a field, you can add descriptive messages to display onscreen by setting the ControlTip Text property for a control. ControlTip text appears when the user points to the control. Setting control tips helps to provide explanations for controls.

In this exercise, you will create control tips for the disabled and locked fields on the Customer Invoices form to explain why they are inaccessible.

1. Display the **Customer Invoices** form in **Design View**.
2. Click the **InvNum** text box and then click the **Other** tab on the Property Sheet.
3. Click in the **ControlTip** text box and type **Invoice Numbers are assigned automatically and cannot be changed.**

4. Enter the following control tips for the following subform controls:

ProdID text box: **Product IDs are assigned by supervisors and cannot be edited.**

Price text box: **Product prices cannot be changed.**

5. Choose **File→Save** or click the **Save** button to save the changes to the form.

6. Switch to **Form View** and point to the InvNum field to display the control tip.

7. Point to the ProdID and Price fields in the subform and notice the control tips do not appear.

Control tips do not display if the subform is in Datasheet View as it currently is.

8. Open the **Customer InvoiceDetails** subform in Form View and point to the ProdID and Price controls to display the control tips.

9. Close Customer InvoiceDetails subform.

Leave the Customer Invoices form open, as you will continue to use it.

Creating a Pop-Up Form

Both forms and reports can be set to open in pop-up windows that stay on top of other open database objects. Pop-up forms can prompt a user for information or display a window containing supplemental data. Such forms or reports can help data entry personnel look up data entry values when they are processing orders or looking up the price of an item. You can apply different formats to pop-up forms.

POP-UP WINDOW MODES

Mode	Description
Modal Pop Up	Displays a custom dialog box that prevents you from accessing other database objects until the dialog box is closed or its required actions are taken.
	Example: The Print dialog box is modal. If you choose to print a report and have the Print dialog box open, you cannot make changes to the report until you click OK or Cancel in the dialog box.
Modeless Pop Up	Creates a pop-up window that sits on top of other open windows in such a way that you can continue to work in the database while it is open.
	Example: When processing orders, you could set the Inventory List to open as a modeless pop-up form to ensure you have the correct inventory number.

DEVELOP YOUR SKILLS: A6-D7

In this exercise, you will create and test a pop-up form using the Winchester Web Design Products table.

1. Select the **Pop Up Products** table and launch the Form Wizard.

2. Add all three fields to the Selected Fields list, choose **Datasheet Layout**, and name the form **Pop Up Products List**.

3. Switch to **Design View** and display the Property Sheet.

4. If necessary, choose **Form** from the Selection Type list in the Property Sheet and then click the **Other** tab and set the Pop Up property to **Yes**.

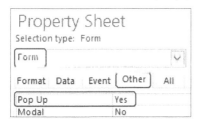

5. Switch to **Datasheet View** and autofit all columns.

6. Change the size of the frame until it just encloses the datasheet.

   You may need to reposition the form first by dragging it so you can see the frame borders.

7. Position the pop-up form in a location where all fields in the Customer Invoices form remain visible.

8. Use the Navigation bar at the bottom of the Customer Invoices form to navigate through the records.

   Notice the pop-up form remains available and in place.

9. Choose **File→Close** to close the database, saving the changes to any unsaved forms.

Self-Assessment

 Check your knowledge of this chapter's key concepts and skills using the Self-Assessment in your ebook or eLab course.

Reinforce Your Skills

Create and Modify a Form with a Subform

In this exercise, you will create a new Donors form for Kids for Change. You will delete, move, and size controls; modify the title; and add a logo to the form.

1. Open **A6-R1-K4C** from your **Access Chapter 6** folder and save it as **A6-R1-K4CRevised**.
2. Select the **Donors** table in the Navigation pane and choose **Create→Forms→Form Wizard** 📖.
3. Add all of the fields from the Donors table to the Selected Fields list, except for the first field, DonorID.

   Hint: The easiest way to do this is to add all of the fields using the Move All Fields >> *button and then use the Remove* < *button to remove the DonorID field.*
4. Click the last field in the Selected Fields list.

   This will ensure that the fields you add in the next step are added to the bottom of the list.
5. Add all four fields from the Donations table to the Selected Fields list.
6. Click **Next** and click **Next** again to leave the viewing options set to **By Donors** and a **Form with Subform(s)**.
7. Leave the layout set to Datasheet and click **Next**.
8. On the final Wizard screen, name the form **Donors Form** and the subform **Donations Subform** and click **Finish**.

   The new form and subform display in Form View.

Adjust the Subform Layout

9. Switch to **Layout View**.
10. Click the *Donations* label to the left of the subform and tap ⌈Delete⌋ to remove it.
11. Double-click the right edge of each subform column heading to autofit the columns.
12. Size the subform by dragging its borders and then use the arrow keys to position the subform as shown here.

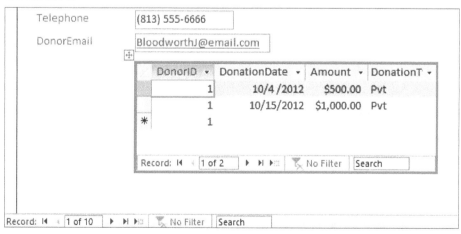

Set Form Field Properties

13. Use the Navigation bar at the bottom of the main form window to navigate to the third record (the McGovern record).

Notice the email address text box is a bit too narrow for the email address.

14. Click the **email address** to select it and then display the Property Sheet.

15. Use the **Format** tab to set the property to to **2.5"**.

16. Use the Navigation bar to scroll through the database records and notice the Acknowledgements text box is larger than it needs to be.

17. Click the **Acknowledgements** text box and set the following properties:

Width: **2"**
Height: **0.5"**

18. Set the widths of the State and DonorZip text boxes to **0.8"**.

Modify the Form Header

19. Click the **Donors Form** title in the Form Header to select the title box.

20. Set the Width property to **3.5"**.

21. Click in the title box and change the title to **Kids for Change Donor Form**.

22. Choose **Design→Header/Footer→Logo** .

23. Navigate to your **Access Chapter 6** folder, choose **K4C-Logo.jpg**, and click **OK**.

24. Set the Width and Height properties to **0.8"** and the Left property to **4"**.

25. Switch to Form View to view your completed form.

26. Choose **File→Close** to close the database, saving the changes to both the form and subform.

REINFORCE YOUR SKILLS: A6-R2

Add a Totals Row to a Form

In this exercise, you will add a Totals row to a form that counts the number of individual donations and totals the amount of the donations.

1. Open **A6-R2-K4C** from your **Access Chapter 6** folder and save it as **A6-R2-K4CRevised**.

2. Select the **Donations Query** in the Navigation pane and launch the **Form Wizard**.

3. Move all of the fields except Acknowledgement, ScholarFund, and NetAmt to the Selected Fields list and click **Next**.

4. Accept the **By Donations** view and click **Next**.

5. Choose the **Datasheet** layout and click **Next**.

6. Name the new form **Total Donations** and click **Finish**.

7. Click the **Select All** box at the top-left corner of the datasheet to select all columns.

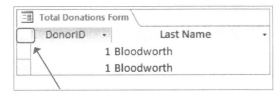

8. Double-click the right edge of any column heading to autofit all of the columns.

9. Choose **Home→Records→Totals** $\boxed{\Sigma}$.

   A Total row is added to the bottom of the datasheet.

10. Click in the **Last Name** cell on the Total row and choose **Count** from the drop-down menu.

    There are 16 individual donations.

11. Click in the **Amount** cell on the Total row and choose **Sum** from the drop-down menu.

12. Autofit the Amount column so the total is visible.

    The donations total $11,150, all in even dollar amounts so decimal places aren't needed.

13. Switch to **Layout View**.

14. Click the **Amount** text box and display the Property Sheet.

15. Set the Decimal Places property on the Format tab to **0** and then close the Property Sheet.

16. Switch to **Datasheet View** and then autofit the Amount column again.

17. Close the database, saving the changes to any unsaved forms.

REINFORCE YOUR SKILLS: A6-R3

Disable and Lock Fields, Calculated Controls, and Pop-Up Forms

In this exercise, you will disable and lock subform fields to prevent information from being altered by those without permission to do so. You will also add a calculated control to a form and create a pop-up form for easy access to donor information.

1. Open **A6-R3-K4C** from your **Access Chapter 6** folder and save it as **A6-R3-K4CRevised**.

2. Display the **Donations** subform in **Design View**.

3. Click the **DonorID** text box and display the Property Sheet.

4. Click the **Data** tab on the Property Sheet and change the Enabled property to **No**.

5. Click the **Other** tab in the Property Sheet and then click in the **ControlTip** text box and type: **Donor IDs are set by the administrator and cannot be edited.**

6. Click in the **Amount** text box on the form and then click the **Data** tab and set the Locked property to **Yes**.

7. Click the **Other** tab and then click in the **ControlTip Text** box and type **Donor Totals are calculated by the program and cannot be edited.**

8. Switch to **Form View** and then point to the DonorID and Amount controls to see the control tips you just created.

9. Close the form, saving the changes.

Create a Calculated Control

10. Choose the **ScholarFund Donations** table in the Navigation pane and then launch the **Form Wizard**.

11. Add all fields to the form and click **Next**.

12. Choose the **Datasheet** layout option and click **Next**.

13. Leave the name as **ScholarFund Donations** and click **Finish**.

14. Switch to **Design View** and then drag the top edge of the **Form Footer** section bar down to make room for a new text box.

15. Choose **Design→Controls→Text Box** [ab|] and then click just below the ScholarFund control to insert a new text box.

16. Use the arrow keys as needed to nudge the control so it is aligned with the ScholarFund control.

17. Make sure the new control is still selected and, if necessary, display the Property Sheet.

18. Click the **All** tab in the Property Sheet and set these four properties:

    Name: **Total Donation**
    Control Source: **=Amount+ScholarFund**
    Format: **Currency**
    Decimal Places: **0**

19. Click the text box label and set the following properties:

    Caption: **Total Donation**
    Width: **1"**
    Left: **0.25"**

20. Switch to **Form View** to see your new calculated control in action.

    Notice the fields are of different widths, creating a poor form layout.

21. Switch back to **Design View** and set the Width property of all of the text boxes to **1"**.

22. Switch back to **Form View**.

    The field widths are now consistent, but the left alignment of the DonationType field needs to be changed.

23. Switch back to **Design View** and set the Text Align property of the DonationType text box to **Right**.

24. Switch back to **Form View** to view your completed form.

Create a Pop-Up Form

25. Choose the **Donors** table in the Navigation pane and launch the **Form Wizard**.

26. Add the **DonorID**, **DonorLName**, and **DonorFName** fields to the Selected Fields list and click **Next**.

27. Choose **Datasheet** layout and click **Next**.

28. Enter **Donor Popup** as the name, choose the option to **Modify the Form's Design**, and then click **Finish**.

    The form displays in Design View.

29. Click the **Other** tab in the Property Sheet and set the Pop Up property to **Yes**.

30. Choose **File→Save** to save the change to the form and then switch to **Datasheet View**.

31. Autofit the three columns in the pop-up form.

32. Adjust the height and width of the pop-up form by dragging the frame borders until the datasheet fits nicely within the frame.

    You may need to drag the form slightly by the title bar prior to sizing it.

33. Now drag the pop-up form to the right of the ScholarFund Donations fields.

34. Navigate through the records in the ScholarFund Donations form and the pop-up form remains in place, giving you all the donor information at a glance.

35. Choose **File→Close** to close the database, saving changes to any unsaved forms.

 Apply Your Skills

Create a Form and Subform and Add a Totals Row

Universal Corporate Events, Ltd., has asked you to create a form with a subform, as well as a quick form that counts salaried employees and totals and averages the salaries.

1. Open **A6-A1-UCE** from your **Access Chapter 6** folder and save it as **A6-A1-UCERevised**.

2. Select the **Venues** table and start the **Form Wizard**.

3. Move all the fields from the Venues table to the Selected Fields list except VenueLiaison.

4. Choose the **Schedules** table in the Tables/Queries list.

5. Move all the fields from the Schedules table to the Selected Fields list except Schedules.VenueID.

6. Accept viewing your data **By Venues** and the **Form with Subform(s)** option.

7. Choose **Datasheet** as the layout option.

8. Name the main form **Venue Events** and the subform **Venue Events Subform**.

9. Switch to **Layout View** and use the following guidelines to modify the subform layout:
   - Remove the Venue Events label.
   - Widen the frame enough so that all columns are visible.
   - Autofit all columns.
   - Reduce the frame width until it is just wide enough to contain the datasheet.
   - Nudge the frame to align it with the text boxes on the main form.

10. Close the form, saving the changes to the form and subform.

11. Choose **Salaried Personnel Query** in the Navigation pane and start the **Form Wizard**.

12. Add all of the fields to the Selected Fields list, choose **Datasheet** layout, and name the new form **Salaried Personnel Totals**.

13. Switch to **Design View** and select the **Salary** label and the **SalaryAmt** text box controls.

14. Press [Ctrl]+[C] and then [Ctrl]+[V] to copy and paste a duplicate salary field under the existing label and text box.

    You may need to drag the Form Footer section down slightly to make room for the paste.

15. Change the name of the first *Salary* label to **Total Salaries**.

16. Change the name of the second *Salary* label to **Average Salary**.

17. Switch to **Datasheet View** and autofit all of the columns.

18. Insert a **Totals** row and insert the following functions in the row:

    Count in the *Salaried* field
    Sum in the *Total Salaries* field
    Average in the *Average Salary* field

    Notice the Count function displays 11 records where the Salaried box is checked.

19. Uncheck several Salaried boxes and notice that the function updates the changes.

20. Close the database, saving the changes to any unsaved forms.

Add a Calculated Control to a Form and Change the Form's Layout

In this exercise, you will add a calculated control to a main form by first copying an existing field. Doing this will retain the formatting of the existing field. You will also adjust the size and position of the controls to change the form's appearance.

1. Open **A6-A2-UCE** from your **Access Chapter 6** folder and save it as **A6-A2-UCERevised**.

2. Open the **Event Pricing Entry** form in **Form View**.

    Notice the labels have a raised effect. You will create a calculated control while retaining the formatting of these fields by copying and pasting an existing field.

3. Switch to **Design View**.

4. Select the **Chg/PP** label and the **ChgPP** text box.

5. Press Ctrl+C to copy the controls and Ctrl+V to paste them.

    An identical text box and label appear below the existing text box and label. Also, you may need to drag the Form Footer bar down slightly to make room for the paste.

6. Change the *Chg/PP* label text for the new label to **Total**.

7. In the Data tab of the Property Sheet, change the Control Source property of the new text box to **=Guests*ChgPP**.

8. Change the Width property of all 8 labels to **1"**.

9. Change the Left property of all 8 text boxes to **1.5"**.

10. Switch to **Form View** to view the changes.

11. Navigate through several records to verify that the calculated control is working properly and that the text boxes are wide enough to accommodate all records.

12. Close the database when you have finished, saving the changes to the form.

Create a Pop-Up Form

In this exercise, you will create a pop-up form to help facilitate data entry.

1. Open **A6-A3-UCE** from your **Access Chapter 6** folder and save it as **A6-A3-UCERevised**.

2. Select the **Events** table and launch the **Form Wizard**.

3. Move both the **EventID** and **EventName** fields to the Selected Fields list, choose the **Tabular** layout, and name the form **Events Pop Up**.

4. Switch to **Design View**.

5. Delete the *Events Pop Up* title in the Form Header section.

6. Set the Top property to **0.1"** for the Event ID label and the Event Name text box in the Form Header.

7. Set the Form Header Height property to **0.4"**.

8. Choose **Form** from the Selection Type drop-down list at the top of the Property Sheet.

9. Set the Pop Up property located in the **Other** tab to **Yes**.

10. Switch to **Form View**.

11. Display the **Venue Events** form in **Form View** and move the pop-up form so you can view the data in the Venue Events form and subform.

    You can see what each Event ID on the Venue Events subform means by looking on the Events Pop Up form.

12. Close the database when you have finished, saving the changes to the form.

 Extend Your Skills

These exercises challenge you to think critically and apply your new skills. You will be evaluated on your ability to follow directions, completeness, creativity, and the use of proper grammar and mechanics. Save files to your chapter folder. Submit assignments as directed.

A6-E1　That's the Way I See It

You've been asked to create a form with a subform in the Blue Jean Landscaping database. Open **A6-E1-BJL** and save it as **A6-E1-BJLRevised**. Use the Form Wizard to create a Blue Jean Landscaping **Customer Sales** form with a **CustSales Details** subform in datasheet layout that includes: SalesNum and SalesDate from the MerchSales table; CustLastName from the Customers table; ItemName, Manufacturer, and Price from the StoreMerchandise table; and QtySold from the MerchSalesDetails table. Enhance the appearance of the forms and add any features you feel will help facilitate effective data entry.

A6-E2　Be Your Own Boss

You've been asked to create a form with a subform in Blue Jean Landscaping database. Open **A6-E2-BJL** and save it as **A6-E2-BJLRevised**. Use the Form Wizard to create a Merchandise Sales form with a Merchandise Sales subform in datasheet layout that includes: SalesNum and SalesDate from the MerchSales table; ItemName, Manufacturer, and Price from the StoreMerchandise table; and QtySold and InvNum from the MerchSalesDetails table. Enhance the appearance of the forms and add any features you feel will help facilitate effective data entry.

A6-E3　Demonstrate Proficiency

Stormy BBQ is continuing to update its database and now wants to have a more exact record of its merchandising sales. Open **A6-E3-SBQ** and save it as **A6-E3-SBQRevised**. Create a new form using the default form and subform names in datasheet layout that includes: SalesID and SalesDate from the MerchSales table; SKU from the MerchSalesDetails table; Manufacturer, ItemName, and ListPrice from the Merchandise table; QtySold from the MerchSalesDetails table. In the subform, add a calculated control to multiply ListPrice by QtySold to produce a line total. Create a pop-up tabular form using the Merchandise table that displays SKU, ItemName, and ListPrice. Enhance the appearance of the forms as desired.

7 | Creating Complex Queries

In this chapter, you will explore queries designed to enhance the timeliness and accuracy of large relational databases. You will create crosstab queries and use parameter queries that prompt you to enter values to generate or modify records. And you will create action queries to update databases and automate database tasks.

LEARNING OBJECTIVES

- Create a crosstab query
- Create a find unmatched query
- Create a find duplicates query
- Create and run parameter queries
- Create and run action queries

Project: Handling Growing Databases

You are responsible for analyzing the data retrieval processes for the growing Winchester Web Design database. You decide to develop queries to increase the efficiency of data entry and updates and to better analyze data. The tools you will use include crosstab queries for data analysis, parameter queries that prompt the user for input, and action queries to update and maintain the database.

Crosstab Queries

Crosstab queries allow you to easily analyze data. A crosstab query lists the fields to be grouped on the left side of the datasheet. It arranges the fields to be summarized across the top so you can calculate sums, averages, counts, or totals by group and subgroup. For example, if you have a database that contains sales records for your employees, the description of each product they sell, and their total sales for each product, you could create a crosstab query to display the total sales by product for each employee. Such a grouping and summarization might appear as shown in the following illustrations.

Original Data

Employee	Product Description	Line Total
JFW	Secondary Page	$1,200.00
JFW	Image, Custom Designed	$440.00
JFW	Home Page, Nav, CSS, Design	$400.00
MJW	Image, Custom Designed	$560.00
MJW	Home Page, Nav, CSS, Design	$400.00
MJW	Secondary Page	$1,400.00
MJW	Hourly Rate for Modifications	$400.00
JMM	Image, Custom Designed	$240.00
JMM	Secondary Page	$400.00
MJW	Blog, Integrated into Site	$300.00

The original data format is arranged by record.

Reorganized by Crosstab Query

Emp Name	Tot Sales	Home Pg	2nd Page	Blogs	Carts	Images	Hourly
Kramer	$13,680.00	$800.00	$7,600.00	$600.00		$2,520.00	$2,160.00
Mansfield	$10,520.00	$400.00	$4,800.00	$600.00	$1,200.00	$1,680.00	$1,840.00
Waters	$20,080.00	$1,600.00	$10,000.00	$1,200.00	$1,200.00	$2,080.00	$4,000.00
Winchester	$17,100.00	$2,000.00	$8,800.00	$300.00	$800.00	$3,040.00	$2,160.00

Using a crosstab query, you can display the data grouped by employee with totals for the various products.

Both tables and queries can be used as the basis of a crosstab query. Crosstab queries can be created while working with an existing query in Design View and choosing the Crosstab option or they can be created using the Query Wizard.

≡ Design→Query Type→Crosstab 🖽

DEVELOP YOUR SKILLS: A7-D1

In this exercise, you will create a crosstab query that lists each employee and their total invoice amount generated by product.

1. Open **A7-D1-WinWebDesign** from your **Access Chapter 7** folder and save it as **A7-D1-WinWebDesignRevised**.

2. Double-click the **Employee Sales** query to run the query and display the resulting datasheet.

   Notice the query contains line item sales data. Each employee has multiple transactions, and each transaction contains the product description, price, and quantity. The LineTotal field is a calculated field that multiplies the Price times the Qty. You will use this query as the basis for your crosstab query.

3. Close the Employee Sales datasheet.

4. Choose **Create→Queries→Query Wizard** 🖽.

5. Choose **Crosstab Query Wizard** and click **OK**.

6. Choose the **Queries** View option then choose **Query: Employee Sales** from the query list.

7. Click **Next** to accept the Employees Sales query as the basis of your crosstab query.

8. Choose **EmpLastName** from the Available fields list and add it to the Selected Fields list.

   Your crosstab query will display employee last names as row headings in the query results datasheet. Each employee will have a single row with their last name displayed in the first cell of the row and their sales information displayed in the other row cells.

9. Click **Next** and choose **ProdDescription** for the column headings.

   The various product descriptions (Blog, Home Page, Web Page) will appear as column headings.

10. Click **Next** and choose **LineTotal** from the Fields list and then choose **Sum** from the Functions list.

    The crosstab query will examine all transactions in the underlying Employee Sales query and sum up the line totals for each product description. So, for example, a total of all line totals will be created where the product description is Blog and the employee is Kramer.

11. Leave the **Yes, Include Row Sums** option checked and click **Next**.

    Leaving the Yes, Include Row Sums option checked will create one additional column in the datasheet, with a total for each employee. The total will be the sum of all of the cells in the crosstab query datasheet for that employee.

12. Leave the query name as Employee Sales_Crosstab and click **Finish**.

    Take a moment to examine the query results. Repeat the Query Wizard steps again if necessary so you fully understand how the query options produce the resulting datasheet.

13. Close the query when you have finished.

Find Queries

Database tables often contain common fields that are used to link or relate the tables. For example, the product id field from a Products table also appears in an Invoices table so that the invoice displays the appropriate products. Thus, it is important that records entered in one table have a matching record in the related table. For example, an invoice should never list a product that is not in the products table.

Sometimes databases are poorly designed, allowing data to be incorrectly entered. Data is also sometimes imported from other data sources, also resulting in incorrect or duplicate data. Fortunately, Access provides two additional Query Wizard options to help resolve these types of data conflicts.

Find Unmatched Query

The find unmatched query locates records in one table that have no related records in another table. For example, you could create a find unmatched query to ensure that each record in an invoice table has a corresponding record in a Customers or Products table.

Find Duplicates Query

A find duplicates query locates records containing duplicate field values in a single table or query datasheet. For example, you could create a find duplicates query to locate all customers with the same last name in a Customers table or to find all customers located in a particular state or ZIP code.

DEVELOP YOUR SKILLS: A7-D2

In this exercise, you will first create a query to locate records in the Customers table that do not have a matching CustomerID in the Invoices table. You will then create a query to identify records with duplicate customer last names.

1. Choose **Create→Queries→Query Wizard** 📇, choose **Find Unmatched Query Wizard**, and click **OK**.

Create a Find Unmatched Query

2. Click **Next** to choose the Customers table.

   Records from the Customers table will appear in the query results.

3. Choose the **Invoices** table and click **Next**.

   You will set up the query to find records in the Invoices table that do not have a matching customer record in the Customers table. Notice the CustID fields are chosen as the matching fields in the wizard screen. They are automatically chosen because a one-to-many relationship is already set up between these fields in the Customers and Invoices tables.

4. Click **Next** to accept CustID as the matching field.

5. Add **CustLastName**, **CustFirstName**, **CustPhone**, and **CustEmail** to the Selected Fields list.

   These are the fields from the Customers table that will be displayed in the query results. This will produce a contact list of customers who don't have invoices in the system and thus haven't bought products in a while, making them potential prospects for new sales.

6. Click **Next** and then click **Finish** to accept the default query name Access assigns.

   Your query should produce a data set of just 3 records.

7. Close the datasheet after you have finished reviewing it.

Create a Find Duplicates Query

8. Choose **Create→Queries→Query Wizard** 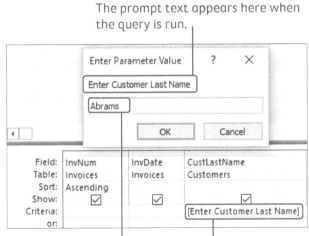.

9. Choose **Find Duplicates Query Wizard** and click **OK**.

10. Click **Next** to choose the Customers table as the query you want to use to search for duplicate field values.

11. Add **CustLastName** to the Duplicate Value Fields list and click **Next**.

    You are only looking for the records of customers who have the same last name.

12. Add **CustFirstName** and **CustPhone** to the Additional Query Fields list and click **Next**.

    These fields will appear in the resulting datasheet but aren't used in the duplicate values test. Only CustLastName is being checked for duplicates.

13. Name the query `Customers with the Same Last Name` and click **Finish**.

    The query results show just two customers with the same last name of Roberts.

14. Close the query when you finished reviewing the results.

Parameter Queries

A parameter query is a select query that prompts the user to enter new criteria values each time the query is run. The query then generates results based on the value(s) entered. For example, a parameter query that searches for customers with a specific last name might prompt the user to enter the desired last name when the query is run. The query then returns only records containing the last name entered by the user. Parameter queries are created by enclosing the desired prompt text with square brackets, [ ], in the query Criteria row.

The prompt text appears here when the query is run.

The user enters the desired parameter value here.

A parameter query is created by enclosing the desired prompt text in square brackets in a Criteria cell.

Customer Invoice Parameter		
InvNum	Invoice Date	Last Name
42	12/6 /2013	Abrams
42	12/6 /2013	Abrams
45	12/18/2013	Abrams

Only records where the customer last name is Abrams are returned.

Complex Parameter Queries

Suppose you want to see all items purchased by a particular customer and those that are equal to or greater than a particular price. For example, all items purchased by Abrams that have a price greater than or equal to $300. This is done by creating an AND condition using parameters in the customer last name and price fields.

Field:	InvNum	InvDate	CustLastName	ProdDescription	Price
Table:	Invoices	Invoices	Customers	Products	Products
Sort:					
Show:	☑	☑	☑	☑	☑
Criteria:			[Enter Customer Name]		>=[Enter Minimum Price]
or:					

A parameter query with two parameters

You can also create expressions with prompts for multiple values in the same query field or include logical criteria such as greater than (>), less than (<), and equal to (=). The following table shows examples of more complex single-field parameter query expressions.

EXAMPLES OF PARAMETER QUERY CRITERIA FOR A SINGLE FIELD

Parameter Criteria	Result
Between [What is the start date?] And [What is the end date?]	Prompts the user to enter a start date and end date. Access recognizes the Between and And expressions and returns dates that are within the range entered by the user.
>=[Enter minimum price]	Displays the prompt "Enter minimum price" and returns only records that are greater than or equal to the price entered by the user.

DEVELOP YOUR SKILLS: A7-D3

In this exercise, you will use parameters to return customer records based on user input.

1. Display the **Customer Invoice Parameter** query in **Design View**.

2. Click in the **CustLastName** criteria field and enter the criterion **[Enter Customer Name]**.

Field:	InvNum	InvDate	CustLastName
Table:	Invoices	Invoices	Customers
Sort:			
Show:	☑	☑	☑
Criteria:			[Enter Customer Name]
or:			

3. Run the query, type **Roberts** in the parameter box that appears, and click **OK**.

All line items from invoices 34 and 7 where the customer last name is Roberts are returned.

Create an AND Parameter Condition

4. Switch to **Design View** and enter the following parameter in the Price criteria box
>=[Enter Minimum Price].

5. Run the query and enter **Roberts** in the first parameter box that appears and **300** in the second box.

Now the record set only has records with Roberts in the last name field where the price is greater than or equal to 300.

6. Close the query, saving the changes.

Action Queries

An action query performs an action that modifies a database table or a group of records in a table. Action queries can modify, move, update, or delete groups of records with a single action. You can even use an action query to create a new table by adding various fields and data from other tables.

An action query is run whenever it is opened. So, if you create an update query designed to increase prices by 10 percent on all items in a table, Access will increase those prices every time you run the query. Action queries do this without opening the underlying tables that are being modified by the query. For this reason, an action query may accidentally be run more than once, inadvertently changing the underlying table data multiple times. Thus, it is good practice to delete action queries after running them. This will help maintain the validity of the database as changes to the underlying data cannot easily be undone.

Action queries require that content within a database be enabled. As a result, if you did not click the Enable Content button found at the top of the Access window when you first opened the database, Access will display an error message advising you to enable content before you can create or run action queries.

> ⚠ **SECURITY WARNING** Some active content has been disabled. Click for more details. | Enable Content |

Make Table Queries

A make table query is an action query that can create a new table using data from multiple database tables. It's also a great way to move data produced from a calculated query field into a table. When you create a new table using a make table query, Access prompts you for a table name and even allows you to save the data in another database. A reason to move records to another database, for example, would be in order to archive them when they become obsolete, such as when a product is no longer available. If you rerun a make table query, Access will replace the table that was created with the previous running of the query. To retain the previously created table you must first rename it so that it isn't replaced.

≡ Design→Query Type→Make Table

DEVELOP YOUR SKILLS: A7-D4

In this exercise, you will create a make table action query to save all of the 2012 invoice records in a new table.

1. Open **Invoices Query** in **Design View**.

2. Enter **Between 1/1/2012 And 12/31/2012** as the criteria for the InvDate field.

   This criterion will produce a datasheet with old invoices that are no longer needed in the database. You'll then use the make table query feature to move the records to a new table.

3. Choose **Design→Query Type→Make Table**.

4. Enter **2012 Invoices** as the table name and click **OK**.

5. **Run !** the query and choose **Yes** to paste 61 rows into a new table.

   The new table named 2012 Invoices appears at the top of the Tables section in the Navigation pane.

6. Open the new **2012 Invoices** table in **Datasheet View**.

   Notice that all of the line items listed have a 2012 invoice date.

7. Close the 2012 Invoices table then close the invoices query without saving the changes.

   It's important not to save the query because it is used for other purposes and because you want to preserve the new table without risking an overwrite of it.

8. Now open the **Invoices** table in **Datasheet View**.

   Notice the Invoices table still contains the 2012 records. Make table queries don't remove data from the underlying tables. They simply copy the data to new tables.

9. Close the Invoices table.

Append Queries

An append query adds a group of records from one or more tables to the end of one or more tables in the same or in another database. For example, if you want to offer a new set of products, you could use an append action query to add the new items from a new products table to the existing products table. Or you might use an append query to automatically add new customers to the Customers table the first time a customer places an order.

Formatting the Source and Destination Tables

In an append query, the table that records are drawn from is called the source table. The table receiving the records is the destination table. To successfully run an append query, the structures, field names, data types, and field order for both tables should be the same.

Identifying the Source and Destination Tables

Append queries are created in the database that contains the source table. When the query is run, the Append dialog box prompts you to identify the destination database and table. Access identifies the destination table in the Append To row of the query grid.

≡ Design→Query Type→Append ⊞

DEVELOP YOUR SKILLS: A7-D5

In this exercise, you will create an action query to append records from the New Products table to the existing Products table.

1. Open the **Products** table and notice that it contains 6 records.
2. Open the **NewProducts** table to see the 5 records that will be appended to the Products table.

    Notice the tables have the same field structure.

3. Close both tables.
4. Choose **Create→Queries→Query Design** ⊞ to create a new query.
5. Add the **New Products** table to the query window and then close the Show Table box.
6. Add all fields from the New Products table to the query grid.
7. Choose **Design→Query Type→Append** ⊞.
8. Click the **Table Name menu** button ▼, choose **Products**, and click **OK**.

    Notice an Append To row has been added to the query. When you run the query, it will copy all records from the underlying New Products table to the Products table. The tables have identical field structures, so the data will drop right into the existing table.

Field:	ProdID	ProdDescription	Price
Table:	New Products	New Products	New Products
Sort:			
Append To:	ProdID	ProdDescription	Price
Criteria:			
or:			

9. **Run** ! the query and choose **Yes** to append the 5 rows to the Products table.

    Nothing appears to happen when you run the query. You can only see the changes after you open the destination table to which the records were appended. Don't run the query again! If you do, Access will add the same records to the destination table again.

10. Display the **Products** table in **Datasheet View** to verify that the new records were appended.

    The Products table should now contain 11 records.

11. Close the Products table.
12. Close the new append query, saving it as **Append Products**.

ACCESS

Update Queries

An update query is an action query that makes global changes to a group of records in one or more tables. For example, you can use an update query to increase the prices for every product in a specific category or to update the area code for phone numbers that change when the phone company adds or changes an area code. To ensure that the corresponding fields in related tables are updated consistently, check the Cascade Update Related Fields checkbox in the Edit Relationships window.

Identifying the Query Grid Update Row

Append, update, crosstab, and delete queries all add a query-specific row to the query grid. The update query places an Update To row in the query grid so that you can tell Access how to update the desired field(s). In most cases, this will be changing one value to another by substitution, mathematical operation, formula, or comparison.

 Design→Query Type→Update

---

DEVELOP YOUR SKILLS: A7-D6

In this exercise, you will create an update action query that increases the prices of every item in the Products table by 10 percent.

1. Open the **Products** table in **Datasheet View** and notice the Home Page price is $400.

   The update query will increase this and all other prices by 10 percent.

2. Close the Products table.

3. Choose **Create→Queries→Query Design**.

4. Add the **Products** table to the query window and then close the Show Table box.

5. Add all fields from the Products table to the query grid.

6. Choose **Design→Query Type→Update**.

   An Update To row is added to the query grid.

7. Click in the **Update To** cell for the Price field and enter **[Price]*1.1**.

   It's important that you include the square brackets, [ ], when entering this formula, otherwise Access will not recognize Price as a field. Multiplying by 1.1 increases the price by 10%.

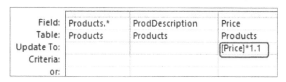

Field:	Products.*	ProdDescription	Price
Table:	Products	Products	Products
Update To:			[Price]*1.1
Criteria:			
or:			

8. **Run** the query and choose **Yes** when the warning prompt appears.

9. Close the query without saving it.

   Once again, it is good practice not to save action queries, such as update queries. Running a query by accident can corrupt data, and recovering corrupted data is often difficult or impossible to do.

10. Open the **Products** table in **Datasheet View** and notice the Home Page price went from $400 to $440 (an increase of 10%).

11. Close the Products table.

Delete Queries

A delete query deletes a group of records from one or more tables. For example, you could create a delete query to remove records for a discontinued line of products or to delete records you have appended to another table to prevent inadvertently running an append query multiple times.

Preparing for Delete Queries

To ensure that corresponding records in related tables will all be deleted concurrently, check the Cascade Delete Related Records checkbox in the Edit Relationships window. When you set up a delete query, Access replaces the Sort row of the query grid with a Delete row. You can set criteria for specific fields in a table to identify the conditions that must be met in order to delete records, or you can set no criteria to remove all records from a table.

 Design→Query Type→Delete

---

DEVELOP YOUR SKILLS: A7-D7

In this exercise, you will create a delete query to remove the 2012 invoices from the Invoices table.

1. Open the **Invoices** table in **Datasheet View**.

   Notice the table still has invoices dated from 2012. These invoices were copied to the 2012 Invoices table using a make table query in a previous exercise. However, make table queries do not delete records, so you'll take care of this using a delete query.

2. Close the Invoices table.

3. Choose **Create→Queries→Query Design**.

4. Add the **Invoices** table to the query window and then close the Show Table box.

5. Add only the **InvDate** field to the query grid.

6. Enter **Between 1/1/2012 and 12/31/2012** as the criteria for the InvDate field.

7. Choose **Design→Query Type→Delete**.

   A Delete row is added to the query grid.

8. **Run** the query and choose **Yes** when the prompt to delete 19 rows appears.

   A second warning prompt appears, notifying you that the records cannot be deleted because there is a key violation. This is occurring because the Cascade Deleted Records option is not activated for a relationship between the Invoices and Invoice Details table. This option must be activated in order for you to run delete queries. You will resolve this in the next few steps.

9. Choose **No** in the warning message box.

10. Choose **Database Tools→Relationships→Relationships**.

11. Right-click the **join line** between the Invoices and Invoice Details table and choose **Edit Relationship**.

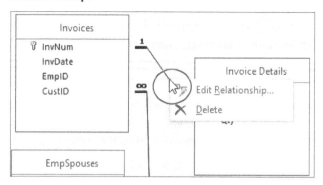

12. Check the **Cascade Delete Related Records** box and click **OK**.

13. Close the Relationships window, saving the changes to the relationship layout.

14. **Run** ![!] the query again, choosing **Yes** when the warning prompt appears.

This time the delete query is able to run, removing the 2012 records from the Invoices table.

15. Close the query without saving it.

Once again, it is good practice not to save action queries, especially when they are relatively easy to recreate, as in this example.

16. Open the **Invoices** table in **Datasheet View** and notice the 2012 invoices have been removed.

17. Close the Invoices table.

18. Choose **File→Close** to close the database.

Self-Assessment

Check your knowledge of this chapter's key concepts and skills using the Self-Assessment in your ebook or eLab course.

Reinforce Your Skills

REINFORCE YOUR SKILLS: A7-R1

Create Crosstab and Find Queries

Kids for Change is planning to fine-tune their database. In this exercise, you will create a crosstab query to track donations and find queries to locate problem records.

1. Open the **A7-R1-K4C** database from your **Access Chapter 7** folder and save it as **A7-R1-K4CRevised**.
2. Launch the **Query Wizard**.
3. Choose **Crosstab Query Wizard** in the first screen and click **OK**.
4. Choose the **Queries** view, choose **Donations Query** as the query that contains the fields you want in the results, and then click **Next**.
5. In the next Wizard screen, move **DonorLName** to the Selected Fields list and click **Next**.

   Donor last names will become your row headings and the field that results are grouped on.

6. In the next Wizard screen, choose only **DonationDate** as the field to appear in the column headings and click **Next**.

   Because DonationDate is a date field, the Wizard asks you to choose an interval. For example, you could have results organized by day, month, or year.

7. Choose **Month** as the interval and click **Next**.
8. Choose **Amount** in the Fields list and **Sum** in the Functions list to identify the field that contains values and the function you want to use.
9. Click **Next**, leave the query name unchanged, and then finish the query.

   The query returns the total donations for each donor, organized by month.

10. Close the query.

Create a Find Unmatched Records Query

11. Launch the **Query Wizard**, choose **Find Unmatched Query Wizard**, and click **OK**.
12. Choose the **Activities** table and click **Next**.

    The Activities table will display in the query results.

13. Choose **Volunteers** as the table with related records and click **Next**.
14. Choose **Day** in the Activities table field list and **VolDay** in the Volunteers table field list and then click **Next**.
15. Add **Activity**, **Day**, and **MeetTime** to the Selected fields list and then click **Next**.
16. Click **Finish** to accept the default query name.

    Your query should return 4 records of activities that do not have a matching volunteer assigned to them.

17. Close the query when you have finished viewing the results.

Create a Find Duplicates Query

18. Launch the **Query Wizard**, choose **Find Duplicates Query Wizard**, and click **OK**.

19. Choose **Donors** as the table to check for duplicates and click **Next**.

20. Add **DonorLName** to the Duplicate-Value Fields list and click **Next**.

You are only looking for records of donors with the same last name.

21. Add **DonorFName** and **DonorPhone** to the Additional Query Fields list and click **Next**.

22. Accept *Find Duplicates for Donors* as the default query name and click **Finish**.

The query should return records for Clay Boltwood and Nancy Boltwood.

23. Close the database, saving the changes, if necessary, to any unsaved queries.

REINFORCE YOUR SKILLS: A7-R2

Create a Parameter Query

In this exercise, you will make a copy of an existing query and then you will modify the new query, turning it into a parameter query to return donor records by state.

1. Open the **A7-R2-K4C** database from your **Access Chapter 7** folder and save it as **A7-R2-K4CRevised**.

2. Click **Donations Query** in the Navigation pane to select it.

3. Press Ctrl + C to copy and Ctrl + V to paste the copy.

4. Enter **Donations by State** as the new query name and click **OK**.

5. Display the **Donations by State** query in **Design View**.

6. Type **[Enter State Abbreviation]** in the **Criteria** cell of the DonorST field and tap Enter to complete the entry.

Field:	DonorID	DonorLName	DonorFName	DonorStreet	DonorCity	DonorST
Table:	Donations	Donors	Donors	Donors	Donors	Donors
Sort:	Ascending					
Show:	☑	☑	☑	☑	☑	☑
Criteria:						[Enter State Abbreviation]
or:						

7. Run [!] the query.

8. Type **MA** when the Parameter Value prompt box appears and click **OK**.

Only donations from Massachusetts donors are returned.

9. Close the query, saving the changes.

10. Choose **File→Close** to close the database and click **Yes** if an empty the Clipboard message appears.

Create Action Queries

In this exercise, you will create a make table query that produces a table to archive the records for the 2012 donations to Kids for Change, a query that appends new records to the Children table, an update query that reduces the duration of each activity by half, and a query that deletes old donations from the Donations table.

1. Open the **A7-R3-K4C** database from your **Access Chapter 7** folder and save it as **A7-R3-K4CRevised**.

Create a Make Table Query

2. Open **Donations Query** and switch to **Design View**.

3. Scroll to the right in the query grid and type **Between 1/1/2012 And 12/31/2012** in the Criteria cell of the DonationDate field.

4. Choose **Design→Query Type→Make Table** 📋.

5. Type **2012 Donations** as the name of the new table and click **OK**.

6. Run the query and choose **Yes** when the warning message appears.

7. Open the **2012 Donations** table to verify that the 2012 donations records are present in the table.

8. Close the 2012 Donations table and then close the Donations Query without saving the changes.

Create an Append Query

9. Open the **Children** table and notice, in the record navigation bar at the bottom of the table grid, that it currently contains 17 records.

10. Close the Children table.

11. Choose **Create→Queries→Query Design** 📋 to create a new query.

12. Add the **NewChildren** table to the query window and then close the Show Table box.

13. Add all fields from the NewChildren table to the query grid in the same order they appear in the NewChildren table box.

14. Choose **Design→Query Type→Append** ➕!.

15. Click the **Table Name menu** button ▼, choose **Children**, and click **OK**.

    The Append To row is added to the query grid

16. **Run** ! the query and choose **Yes** to add the 10 records to the Children table.

17. Close the query, saving it as **Append New Children**.

18. Open the **Children** table; it should now have 27 records.

19. Close the Children table.

Create an Update Query

20. Display the **Activities** table in **Datasheet View** to see the current Hrs values.

The current activities last either 2 or 4 hours.

21. Close the Activities table

22. Choose **Create→Queries→Query Design** ⊞.

23. Add the **Activities** table and close the Show Table dialog box.

24. Add the **Hours** field to the query grid.

25. Choose **Design→Query Type→Update** ⊿!.

An Update To row is added to the query.

26. Type **[Hours]/2** in the **Update To** cell of the Hours field.

It's important to include the square brackets so that Access can perform the correct calculation. This calculation will divide the current activity hours value in half.

27. **Run** ! the query and choose **Yes** to update 25 rows.

28. Close the query without saving it.

29. Open the **Activities** table and note the activities that were listed as 2 and 4 hours each are now 1 and 2 hours each.

30. Close the Activities table.

Create a Delete Query

31. Open the **Donations** table and notice it contains donations from the year 2012.

32. Close the Donations table.

33. Choose **Create→Queries→Query Design** ⊞.

34. Add the **Donations** table to the query and then close the Show Table dialog box.

35. Double-click the **DonationDate** field to add it to the query grid.

36. Type **Between 1/1/2012 And 12/31/2012** in the Criteria row for the DonationDate field.

37. Choose **Design→Query Type→Delete** ✗.

A Delete row is added to the query grid.

38. **Run** ! the query and choose **Yes** when the deleting 4 records warning message appears.

39. Close the query without saving it.

40. Open the **Donations** table and the 2012 records will be removed.

41. Choose **File→Close** to close the database.

 Apply Your Skills

Create Crosstab and Find Queries

Universal Corporate Events, Ltd., has asked you to create queries to analyze the company's data and identify unmatched and duplicate database records. In this exercise, you will respond to this request by creating crosstab, find unmatched records, and find duplicate records queries.

1. Open the **A7-A1-UCE** database from your **Access Chapter 7** folder and save it as **A7-A1-UCERevised**.

2. Use the **Query Wizard** to create a crosstab query using the following parameters:

View	**Query: Event Revenue**
Row Heading(s)	**VenueID**
Column Heading(s)	**ContactID**
Field(s)	**TotalRev**
Function(s)	**Sum**
Name	**Contact Revenue by Venue**

3. Finish the query.

   Seven data rows should be returned.

4. Close the query.

5. Use the **Query Wizard** to create a find unmatched query using the following parameters:

View	**Table: Venues**
Related Records	**Table: Schedules**
Fields in Venues	**VenueID**
Fields in Schedules	**VenueID**
Fields to see in query results	**VenueName, VenueStreet, VenueCity, VenueST, VenueZIP, VenuePhone, VenueWebSite**
Name	**Venues Without Event Scheduled**

6. Finish the query.

   Three data rows should be returned.

7. Close the query.

8. Use the **Query Wizard** to create a find duplicates query using the following parameters:

View	**Query: Event List**
Duplicate-Value Field	**EventDate**
Additional Fields	**VenueID, ContactID, MenuPlan, Guests**
Name	**Find Double-Booked Dates**

9. Finish the query.

   Two data rows should be returned.

10. Close the database.

Create a Parameter Query

In this exercise, you will create a parameter query to return personnel records by city.

1. Open the **A7-A2-UCE** database from your **Access Chapter 7** folder and save it as **A7-A2-UCERevised**.
2. Create a new query using **Query Design** and add the **Personnel** table to the query.
3. Add the **PerLastName**, **PerFirstName**, **PerAddr**, **PerCity**, **PerPhone**, and **PerEmail** fields to the query.
4. Make **[Enter City]** a Criterion for the PerCity field.
5. Run the query using **Sarasota** as the parameter value.

   The query should return 5 records where the city is Sarasota.
6. Close the database, saving the query as **Personnel City**.

Create Action Queries

In this exercise, you will create a make table query to archive the records for older events, an append query to add new records to the Schedules table, and an update query to change personnel salaries. Finally, you will create a query to delete older events from the main Schedules table.

1. Open the **A7-A3-UCE** database from your **Access Chapter 7** folder and save it as **A7-A3-UCERevised**.

Create a Make Table Query

2. Display **Schedules Query** in **Design View** and add the criterion **<01/01/2014** to the EventDate field.
3. Use the **Make Table** query type to create a new table with the name **Older Events**.
4. Run the query.

   The new table should contain 6 records.
5. Close the Schedules Query without saving the changes.

Create an Append Query

6. Open the **Schedules** table and notice there are 42 records.

   In the following steps you will append records to this table.
7. Close the Schedules table.
8. Create a new query adding all of the fields from the **New Schedules** table.
9. Use the **Append** query type to convert the query to an append query using **Schedules** as the table name to append to.

10. Run the query, choosing **Yes** when asked if you wish to add the 30 rows to the Schedules table.

11. Close the query, saving it as **Append Schedules**.

12. Open the **Schedules** table.

    It should now contain 72 records.

13. Close the Schedules table.

Create an Update Query

14. Open the **SalaryGrades** table in **Datasheet View** and take a moment to review the current salaries.

    In the next few steps, you will create an update query that increases all salaries by 7%.

15. Close the SalaryGrades table.

16. Create a new query using the **SalaryGrades** table and adding only the **SalaryAmt** field to the query grid.

17. Use the **Update** query type to add an Update row to the query.

18. Use an update criterion that multiplies the **SalaryAmt** field by **1.07**.

    This will produce the 7% increase.

19. Run the query, choosing **Yes** to update 21 records.

20. Close the query, saving it as **Salary Updates**.

21. Open the **SalaryGrades** table to verify that the salaries have indeed been updated.

22. Close the SalaryGrades table.

Create a Delete Query

23. Open the **Schedules** table and notice it still contains records with Event Dates that are prior to 2014.

24. Close the Schedules table.

25. Create a new query using only the **EventDate** field from the Schedules table.

26. Use the criterion **<1/1/2014** in the **EventDate** field.

27. Use the **Delete** query type and then run the query, choosing **Yes** to delete 6 records.

28. Close the new query without saving it.

29. Open the **Schedules** table to verify that all records with Event Dates prior to 1/1/2014 have been deleted.

30. Close the database.

 Extend Your Skills

These exercises challenge you to think critically and apply your new skills. You will be evaluated on your ability to follow directions, completeness, creativity, and the use of proper grammar and mechanics. Save files to your chapter folder. Submit assignments as directed.

A7-E1   That's the Way I See It

You've been asked to provide several enhancements to the Blue Jean Landscaping database. Open **A7-E1-BJL** and save it as **A7-E1-BJLRevised**. Make a copy of the Service Invoices Query, name it **Acre Rate Range**, and then modify the Acre Rate Range query to add a parameter that prompts the user to enter the rate per acre the user wants to know about. The query should only return records that match the acre rate entered by the user. The second update is to the StoreMerchandise table. Create an append query named **New Merchandise** that appends all of the records from the NewMerchandise table to the StoreMerchandise table. Verify that your queries are functioning properly.

A7-E2   Be Your Own Boss

Business has picked up at Blue Jean Landscaping, and you must modify the database to ensure it is more efficient and can cope with unexpected situations. Open **A7-E2-BJL** and save it as **A7-E2-BJLRevised**. Use the Store Inventory query as the basis for a new query named **Manufacturer Item Inventory** that prompts the user to enter a manufacturer and returns all of the records for that manufacturer. Create a query named **2013 Sales** to create a new table containing all of the 2013 sales records from the Merch Sales query. Finally, create an append query named **New Customers** that appends all records from the NewCustomers table to the Customers table.

A7-E3   Demonstrate Proficiency

Stormy BBQ has asked you to make a number of refinements to the merchandising section of its database. Open **A7-E3-SBQ** and save it as **A7-E3-SBQRevised**. Create a query to copy the 2013 merchandise sales records from the MerchSales table into a new table and then create a delete query to remove those records from the MerchSales query. Decide what names to assign to the new table and to either of the two queries you choose to save. Create a query that increases the List Price of all of the items in the Merchandise table by 5%. You decide whether or not to save the query after running it and which name to use if you decide to save it.

8 | Customizing Reports

Database reports summarize
the data contained in tables or
displayed in query results and
able you to provide information in a page
yout suitable for printing. Although forms
d reports serve two different purposes
thin the context of a relational database, the
chniques used to customize them are similar.
this chapter, you will import reports from
her databases and use features to create
stom reports.

LEARNING OBJECTIVES

- Import a report into a database
- Add a subreport to a main report
- Create a report from a subreport
- Create calculated controls on a subreport
- Set page breaks in reports

📂 Project: Billing Customers

The company manager of Winchester Web Design, a small web page design company, wants you to improve its invoice report for customer billing. After reviewing invoices from several companies, the company manager has sketched out a design for the new invoice report layout. Your job is to create a sample of the new invoice report for the company's executive team.

Importing a Report into a Database

Access offers a variety of ways to create reports. In addition to using the Report Wizard or starting from scratch in Design View, you can also import reports from another database. Because most companies require some type of invoice to send with customer orders, locating a sample invoice report to import is not difficult.

Sometimes you have the report you want, but during its design it may have become corrupted, either due to inadvertent changes to the report itself or because of changes to an underlying query. That's when backups are invaluable. If a report becomes corrupted, you can restore it by importing database objects from a backup copy of a database. The record source should already match, and there should be no need to edit the properties or the field names.

Identifying Report Record Sources

Reports that you import retain two connections to their original database. The first is the source database table or query name, shown in the Record Source property and the second are the field names, which appear in report text boxes. As a result, when you import a report from another database, you often must establish new control sources to the destination database. You can accomplish this by:

▶ Editing the imported report's Record Source property to link to a table or query in the destination database.

▶ Editing, if necessary, the field names in the imported report's text boxes to match those shown in the new record source table or query.

 External Data→Import & Link→Access 🗗

DEVELOP YOUR SKILLS: A8-D1

In this exercise, you will import a report from a backup copy of a database. You will rename the report and view data from an existing table using the imported report.

1. Open **A8-D1-WinWebDesign** from your **Access Chapter 8** folder and save it as **A8-D1-WinWebDesignRevised**.

2. Look in the Reports section in the Navigation pane and notice the database contains just two reports.

3. Choose **External Data→Import & Link→Access** 🗗.

4. Click **Browse**, navigate to your **Access Chapter 8** folder, choose **A8-D1-WinWebDesign -Backup**, and click **Open**.

   This database is a backup copy of the WinWebDesign database.

5. Leave the storage setting as Import Tables, Queries, Forms, Reports, Macros, and Modules into the Current Database and click **OK**.

   Access opens the Import Objects dialog box and displays object names contained in the backup database in tabbed groups.

6. Click the **Reports** tab, choose **Customer Invoices**, and click **OK**.

7. Leave the Save Import Steps checkbox unchecked and click **Close** in the Get External Data dialog box.

   Notice the Customer Invoices report has been added to the Reports section of the Navigation pane.

8. Double-click the **Customer Invoices** report to open it in **Report View**.

9. If necessary, scroll down and then notice the empty space between the Customer Information and signature blocks.

   This is a great spot to insert a subform/subreport that includes the invoice detail lines.

Adding a Subreport to a Main Report

Subreports display subsets of data in reports and are derived from related database tables, similar to subforms on forms. However, a subreport can display table data by using a table, query, form, or another report as its source object. Forms are frequently created before reports and they often already display the desired data needed in a report. For these reasons, it is often best to use a subform as the basis of a subreport to streamline report design and layout.

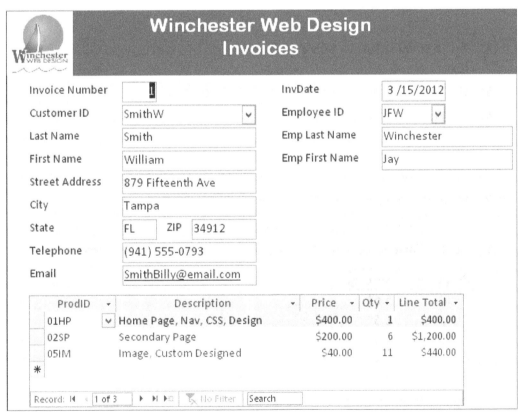

An invoice report that uses a subform to display invoice details

Adding a Subreport

The procedures used to add a subreport to a report are basically the same as those used to add a subform to a form. You can create the subreport using the Report Wizard or add an unbound subreport control to the report. Then you identify the database object containing the fields you want to display as a subreport.

☰ Design→Controls→Subform/Subreport ⊞

DEVELOP YOUR SKILLS: A8-D2

In this exercise, you will add a subreport to the Customer Invoices report. You will use the InvoiceDetails subform as the source for the subreport.

1. Display the **Customer Invoices** report in **Design View**.

Insert a Subform

2. Choose **Design→Controls→Subform/Subreport** ⊞ (located at the bottom of the controls list).

3. Click just below the ZIP label to insert a control and launch the **SubReport Wizard**.

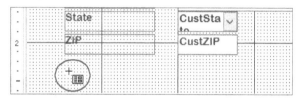

4. Choose **InvoiceDetails Subform** from the Use an Existing Report or Form option and click **Next**.

5. Click **Next** again to accept Choose from a List as the linking method.

6. Click **Finish** to accept InvoiceDetails Subform as the name.

   The subform is inserted in the report.

Set Properties

7. Display the Property Sheet, if necessary, and click the **Data** tab.

   Notice the Source Object is set to Form.InvoiceDetails Subform.

8. Click the **Format** tab in the Property Sheet and set the following properties:

Property	Setting
Width	**5.6"**
Height	**1.5"**
Top	**2.9"**
Left	**0.5"**

9. Click the **InvoiceDetails Subform** label, which should be just below the ZIP label, and set the following properties:

Label	Property
Caption	**Invoice Details**
Width	**1.2"**
Height	**0.25"**
Top	**2.5"**
Left	**0.5"**
Font Name	**Arial Rounded MT Bold**
Font Size	**10**
Fore Color	**Blue, Accent 1, Darker 50%**

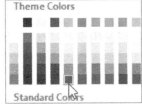

10. Switch to **Report View** to see your completed report.

11. Use the record Navigation bar and the scroll bar to review the database records.

Notice the information in both the report and the subform changes each time a new record is displayed.

12. Close the report, saving the changes.

Creating a Report from a Subreport

Using a subform as the record source for a subreport is convenient because the subform already includes all of the needed data. However, when a subreport uses a form as the record source, any changes made to the subreport layout are reflected in the source form. If you don't want the source form to be changed, you can save the subreport as a separate report in the database, change the main report's Record Source property to the new report object, and then edit the subreport.

Access allows you to save an existing form as a new form, and an existing report as a new report. When a subform is used as the record source for a subreport, you can open the subreport in a separate window and save it as a separate report.

≣ File→Save As→Save Object As

In this exercise, you will create and save a new report based on the subreport from the Customer Invoice Report. You will then edit the source object property in the main report to display the new subreport.

1. Open **InvoiceDetails Subform** from the Forms section of the Navigation pane.

Use the Subform to Create a Subreport

2. Choose **File→Save As→Save Object As→Save As**.

3. Type **WWD Customer Invoices Subreport** as the name, choose **Report** from the **As** drop-down list, and click **OK**.

   A new report is added to the Reports section of the Navigation pane.

4. Close InvoiceDetails Subform.

5. Open the new **WWD Customer Invoices Subreport** in Design View.

6. Display the Property Sheet, if necessary.

7. Click the **All** tab and type **Customer Invoices Subreport** as the caption.

Create a Title for the Subreport

8. Choose **Design→Header/Footer→Title**.

   Access places a title and empty placeholder controls in the Report Header.

9. Type **Winchester Web Design Invoice Details** in the title control and tap ⌈Enter⌋.

10. Set the following property values for the new title control:

Property	Setting
Width	**3"**
Height	**0.25"**
Left	**1"**
Font Name	**Arial**
Font Size	**12**
Text Align	**Center**

11. Click the **Report Header** section bar and set the Height property to **0.3"**.

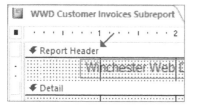

Inserting the title in the Report Header had the effect of widening the subreport, so you will now reset the width back to 5.6".

12. Click the **Report Selector** button and set the Width property to **5.6"**.

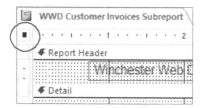

13. Close the subreport, saving the changes.

14. Open the **Customer Invoices** report in **Design View**.

15. If necessary, display the Property Sheet and click the **Data** tab.

16. Click on the **subreport** to select it.

17. Click in the **Source Object** property box and choose **Report.WWD Customer Invoices Subreport** from the drop-down menu.

18. Switch to **Report View** to see how the new subreport looks.

    Notice the change in appearance when compared with the subform that was used previously.

19. Scroll through the report, seeing how the subreport always shows the correct invoice details.

20. Close the Customer Invoices report, saving the changes.

Numbering Items in a Report

As the number of records in a table grows, the length and number of records in a report or subreport also grows. You can number the records in a report to help track the items listed. If a report is grouped, you can set the count to restart numbering at the beginning of each group.

Setting Properties to Number Items

By adding a text box to the Detail section and setting its Control Source property to *=1*, you can automatically number items in a report. In addition, you can set the Running Sum property to identify the portion of a report for which you want to count items. For example, suppose you have an invoice report that groups services by invoice number. You can set the Running Sum property to count the items in each group and then start counting again with the next group.

Numbering Subreports Separately

Access does not permit numbering items in a subreport control on a main report. However, because you saved the subreport as a separate report, you can add the numbering controls directly to the subreport by opening it in a separate window. Any edits you make when it is open as a separate item are reflected in the main report the next time you open it.

DEVELOP YOUR SKILLS: A8-D4

In this exercise, you will reposition the controls in the Page Header of the WWD Customer Invoices Subreport and then add a text box control to count the number of line items.

1. Display the **WWD Customer Invoices Subreport** in **Design View**.

2. Right-click the **Detail** section bar and choose **Page Header/Footer**.

   You will add labels to the Page Header.

3. Click the **Page Header** section bar and change the Height property to **0.3"**.

4. Select the **ProdID** label in the Detail section and use Ctrl + X to cut the control.

5. Click in the **Page Header** section and use Ctrl + V to paste the label.

6. With the **ProdID** label still selected, set both the Width and Left properties to **0.5"**.

7. Use the procedure in steps 4–6 to move the **Description**, **Price**, **Qty**, and **LineTotal** labels one at a time into the Page Header section, setting the Width and Left properties as follows:

Property	Width Setting	Left Setting
Description	2"	1.25"
Price	0.75"	3.5"
Qty	0.3"	4.5"
LineTotal	0.75"	5"

8. If necessary, click on the labels and use the up arrow ⬆ key to nudge them up until they are vertically aligned with the ProdID label as shown here.

```
✦ Page Header
        ProdID:    Description                              Price    Qty    Line Total
✦ Detail
```

Move and Resize Report Text Box Controls

9. Set these property values for the text boxes in the **Detail** section:

Text Box Control	Width	Top	Left
ProdID	0.5"	0.1"	0.5"
ProdDescription	2"	0.1"	1.25"
Price	0.75"	0.1"	3.5"
Qty	0.3"	0.1"	4.5"
LineTotal	0.75"	0.1"	5"

10. Click the **Detail** section bar and set the Height property to **0.5**".

11. Click the **Selection Type menu** button ▼ at the top of the Property Sheet and choose **Report**.

12. Set the Width property to **6**".

13. Switch to **Report View**.

There is room for a small field to the left of the ProdID field, which is where you will insert numbering.

Add and Format a Text Box

14. Switch to **Design View** and choose **Design→Controls→Text Box** ⌨.

15. Click to the left of the *ProdID* text box in the Detail section to position the new box in that area.

The precise location is not important, as you will set the position , using specific properties, in a moment.

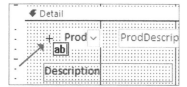

16. Click the label of the new text box and tap ⎯Delete⎯ to remove it.

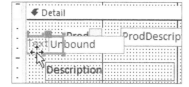

17. Click the new text box control and set these property values using the **All** tab in the Property Sheet:

Property	Setting
Name	**txtCount**
Width	**0.3"**
Top	**0.1"**
Left	**0.1"**

Set Control Properties to Sum

18. Click the **Data** tab and set the Control Source property to **=1** and the Running Sum property to **Over Group**.

19. Switch to **Report View** and scroll through the report.

Notice that the numbering continues sequentially throughout the report.

20. Close the WWD Customer Invoices Subreport, saving the changes.

21. Display the **Customer Invoices** report in **Design View**.

22. Click the **InvoiceDetails Subform** to select it and set the Width property to **6"**.

23. Switch to **Print Preview** and use the Navigation bar to review the various report pages.

Notice that each invoice begins on a new page and that the invoice detail line items begin at number 1 for each invoice.

24. Close Print Preview and then close the Customer Invoices report, saving the changes.

Creating Calculated Controls on a Subreport

Reports summarize data contained in tables and queries to present useful, organized information. This typically means that calculated fields must be added to a report for subtotals, grand totals, and averages.

Positioning Calculated Controls

Calculated controls are built in reports by using the Control Source property of an unbound text box control to which you add a formula. The placement of the calculated control determines how Access performs the calculation.

Calculated control in a Detail section
performs a calculation for each detail line.

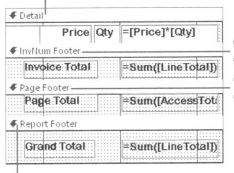

Calculated control in a Group Footer
calculates the total for the group.

Calculated control in a Page Footer
calculates the total for the page.

Calculated control in a Report Footer
calculates the total for the entire report.

DEVELOP YOUR SKILLS: A8-D5

In this exercise, you will add a calculated control to the Report Footer section of the WWD Customer Invoices Subreport.

1. Display the **WWD Customer Invoices Subreport** in **Design View**.
2. Click the **Report Footer** section bar and set the Height property to **0.3"**.
3. Choose **Design→Controls→Text Box** ⌗.
4. Click anywhere in the **Report Footer** section.
5. Click the **All** tab in the Property Sheet.
6. Set the following properties for the new control:

Property	Setting
Name	**CustomerTotal**
Control Source	**=Sum([Price]*[Qty])**
Format	**Currency**
Height	**0.25"**
Top	**0"**
Left	**4.75"**

7. Click the new text box label and set the following property values:

Property	Setting
Caption	**Invoice Total**
Width	**1.2"**
Height	**0.25"**
Top	**0"**
Left	**3"**
Fore Color	**Text Dark**

8. Close and save the changes to the subreport.
9. Display the **Customer Invoices** report in **Report View**.

   Notice the Invoice Total *label and calculated control you just created.*

Growing a Subreport

When the number of records or amount of data displayed in a subreport varies, you can set the Can Grow property setting to allow the subreport space to expand so more data displays vertically. You can also change the orientation of the print layout to allow more horizontal space on each report page.

DEVELOP YOUR SKILLS: A8-D6

In this exercise, you will adjust the margins of the Customer Invoices report and set the Can Grow and Can Shrink properties. These properties will adjust the size of the subreport to fit the contents.

1. Display the **Customer Invoices** report in **Design View**.
2. Choose **Page Setup→Page Size→Margins→Narrow**.

3. Click on the **InvoiceDetails Subreport** to select it.

4. Click the **Format** tab on the Property Sheet and, if necessary, set both the Can Grow and Can Shrink properties to **Yes**.

5. Choose **File** ›**Save** to save the report.

6. Switch to **Report View** and scroll through the report.

   Notice the subreport grows and shrinks to best fit the contents.

Setting Page Breaks and Customizing Controls

As you view the Winchester Web Design Customer Invoices report in Report View, you may notice that the number of invoice records displayed on each screen varies depending on the number of items ordered. To ensure that each customer invoice starts on a new page, you can add a page break control. By default, when you view a report in Print Preview, data for each customer/record automatically appears on a separate page; however, multiple records appear on the same page when the report is displayed in Report View.

To add a title or general company information to an invoice, place title controls in the Page Header section rather than the Report Header, which only prints on the first page.

Positioning the Page Break Control

To ensure that each invoice record prints on a separate sheet of paper, you can set page breaks. When you set page breaks, add the break at the end of the Detail section so Access knows to start a new page before printing the next page header.

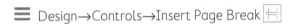 Design→Controls→Insert Page Break

---

DEVELOP YOUR SKILLS: A8-D7

In this exercise, you will modify the Winchester Web Design Customer Invoice Report. You will add a title and the current date and set page breaks to print each invoice on a separate page.

1. Display the **Customer Invoices** report in **Design View**.

Modify the Title

2. Click the **Customer Invoice** title in the Page Header and then click again just in front of *Customer* to position the insertion point there.

3. Type **Winchester Web Design** and then press Shift + Enter to force *Customer Invoice* to a second line.

4. Click in an empty part of the Page Header and then click the title box to select it.

5. Set the Width property to **4"** and the Left property to **2"**.

Add a Date Control

In the next few steps, you will insert a date that will display in the Report Header. You will then remove it from the Report Header and place it in the Page Header so it appears on every page rather than just the first page of the report.

6. Choose **Design→Header/Footer→Date and Time** 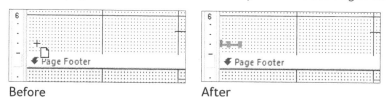.

7. Choose the **MM/DD/YYYY** date format, remove the check from the **Include Time** box, and then click **OK**.

   Access places the new date control in the Report Header section.

8. Select the **date** control and press ☐Ctrl☐+☐X☐ to cut it from the Report Header.

9. Click the **Page Header** section bar and press ☐Ctrl☐+☐V☐ to paste the date into the Page Header.

10. Set the following properties for the date control:

Property	Setting
Width	**2"**
Height	**0.2"**
Top	**0.4"**
Left	**5.8"**

Add a Page Break Control

11. Scroll down to the bottom of the Detail section.

12. Choose **Design→Controls→Insert Page Break** ⊟.

13. Place the page break in the Detail section just above the Page Footer section bar.

Before   After

14. Switch to **Print Preview** and use the Navigation bar to browse the various pages.

    Notice the date appears in each invoice because you added it in the Page Header section. Also notice each invoice begins on a new page. There are times when adding a page break to a report may not be necessary and may cause an unneeded page to print for each record. If this occurs in your report, then remove the page break.

15. Close Print Preview.

16. Choose **File→Close** to close the database and save the changes to the **Customer Invoices** report.

Self-Assessment

Check your knowledge of this chapter's key concepts and skills using the Self-Assessment in your ebook or eLab course.

Reinforce Your Skills

Import a Report and Add a Subreport

In this exercise, you will import a report from the Kids for Change database and then add a subform with details on the activities provided by the staff.

1. Open **A8-R1-K4C** from your **Access Chapter 8** folder and save it as **A8-R1-K4CRevised**.

Import a Report

2. Choose **External Data→Import & Link→Access** .
3. Click **Browse** and navigate to your **Access Chapter 8** folder.
4. Choose **A8-R1-K4C-Backup** and click **Open**.
5. Leave the storage setting as Import Tables, Queries, Forms, Reports, Macros, and Modules into the Current Database and click **OK**.
6. Click the **Reports** tab, choose **Staff Report**, and click **OK**.
7. Leave the Save Import Steps checkbox unchecked and click **Close** in the Get External Data dialog box.
8. Display the newly imported **Staff Report** in **Report View**.

   The empty space between the staff records is where you will insert the subreport.

Add and Format a Subreport

9. Switch to **Design View** and choose **Design→Controls→Subform/Subreport** (you'll need to scroll to the bottom of the controls list).
10. Click just below the *Activity ID* label in the Detail section to insert a control and launch the **Subreport Wizard**.

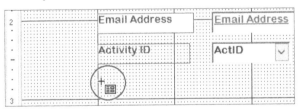

11. Choose **Staffing Subform** from the Use an Existing Report or Form option and click **Next**.
12. Click **Next** again to accept Choose from a List as the linking method.
13. Click **Finish** to accept Staffing Subform as the name.

    A small green triangle in the Report selector indicates a possible error. Clicking the triangle displays a smart tag, which lists the error and possible solutions. In this case, the report is wider than a page. The next few steps will eliminate the error.

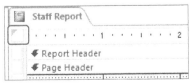

ACCESS

14. Click the *Staffing Subform* label and tap ⌷Delete⌷ to remove it.

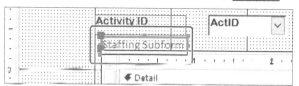

15. Click the **subreport** to select it and then set the following properties:

Property	Setting
Width	**7.7"**
Height	**0.5"**
Top	**3"**
Left	**0"**
Border Style	**Transparent**

16. Click the **Report** selector and set the Width property to **7.8"**.

The green smart tag indicator should be gone now.

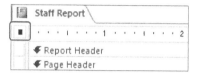

17. Choose **File→Save** to save Staff Report and then switch to **Report View**.

18. Scroll through the report and notice the activity details now appear under the staff information.

19. Close the database.

REINFORCE YOUR SKILLS: A8-R2

Create a Report from a Subreport and Number Report Items

In this exercise, you will save a subreport as a separate report and then also update a report of the donations to Kids for Change, numbering them in order to add a count of the donations per donor.

1. Open **A8-R2-K4C** from your **Access Chapter 8** folder and save it as **A8-R2-K4CRevised**.

Create a Report from a Subreport

2. Open the report named **Staff Report** and then switch to **Design View**.

3. Right-click the **subreport** control and choose **Subreport in New Window**.

The Staffing Subform subreport opens in a separate window.

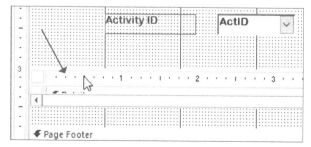

4. Choose **File→Save As→Save Object As→Save As**.

5. Type **K4C Staffing Subreport** as the name, choose **Report** from the Save As drop-down list, and click **OK**.

6. Close the subform and close Staff Report.

7. Display the new **K4C Staffing Subreport** in **Design View**.

8. Click the **Detail** section bar and set the Height property to **0.3"**.

9. Right-click the **Detail** section bar and choose **Report Header/Footer**.

   The Report Header appears.

10. Click the **Report Header** section bar.

11. Click in the **Back Color** property box then click the **Build** ⋯ button.

12. Choose **Blue, Accent 1, Lighter 80%**.

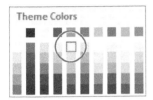

13. Choose **Design→Controls→Label** [Aa] and then click in the **Report Header** section above the ActID control and type **ID** for the new label text.

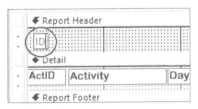

14. Add 6 more labels using the names **Activity, Day, Time, Venue, Street,** and **City**.

    You don't need to be precise with the label positions, as you will modify their properties in the next step.

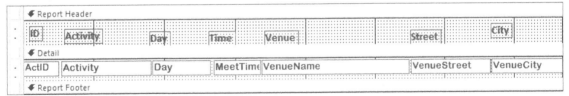

15. Press the ⎡Ctrl⎤ key and click all 7 labels to select them, and then set the following properties:

Property	Setting
Height	0.2"
Top	0"
Font Name	**Arial Rounded MT Bold**
Font Size	**10**
Fore Color	**Blue, Accent 1**

16. Click in an empty spot within the **Report Header** to deselect the labels.

17. If necessary, click the individual labels and widen them slightly until the text is fully visible and then nudge them left or right to align them with the text boxes in the Detail section.

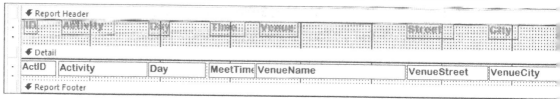

18. Close and save K4C Staffing Subreport.

19. Display **Staff Report** in **Design View**.

20. Click the **subreport** control to select it.

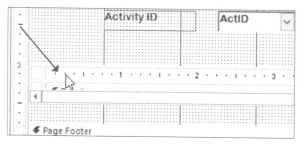

21. Set the following properties using the **All** tab of the Property Sheet:

Name: **Staffing Subreport**
Source Object: **Report.K4C Staffing Subreport**

22. Switch to **Report View** to see the changes you've made.

23. Close and save Staff Report.

Number Report Items

24. Display **Donations Report** in **Design View**.

25. Choose **Design→Controls→Text Box** [abl] and click in the **Detail** section to the left of the DonorID text box.

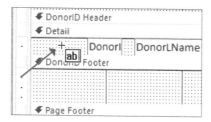

26. Click on the label control for the new text box (it will be to the left of the text box and difficult to see) and then tap ⸢Delete⸣ to remove it.

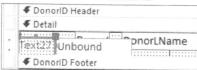

27. Select the new text box control and then set these property values in the **All** tab of the Property Sheet:

Property	Setting
Name	**txtCounter**
Control Source	**=1**
Width	**0.3"**
Top	**0"**
Left	**0.3"**
Border Style	**Transparent**
Font Name	**Arial**
Font Weight	**Semi-Bold**

28. Click the **Data** tab in the Property Sheet and set the Running Sum property to **Over All**.

29. Switch to **Report View**.

Access numbers the detail lines consecutively for each individual donation.

30. Close the database, saving the changes to the Donations Report.

REINFORCE YOUR SKILLS: A8-R3

Calculated Fields and Page Breaks

Kids for Change wants to improve its Monthly Donations Report. In this exercise, you will add a field to calculate the total monthly donations for each donor. You will set the subreport to grow and shrink, and you will add custom controls and a page break.

1. Open **A8-R3-K4C** from your **Access Chapter 8** folder and save it as **A8-R3-K4CRevised**.

Add a Calculated Field to a Report

2. Display **K4C Donors Subreport** in **Design View**.

3. Choose **Design→Controls→Text Box** abl and click in the **Page Footer** section under the Amount text box to place a new text box there.

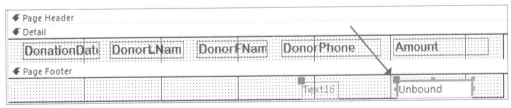

4. Click the text box label and tap Delete to remove it.

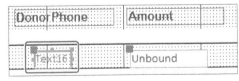

5. Click the new text box and set these properties on the **All** tab of the Property Sheet:

Property	Setting
Name	**MonthTotal**
Control Source	**=Sum([Amount])**
Format	**Currency**
Width	**1.3"**
Height	**0.2"**
Top	**0"**
Left	**5"**
Font Name	**Arial Rounded MT Bold**
Text Align	**Right**

6. Close and save the K4C Donors Subreport.

Grow and Shrink a Subreport

7. Display **Monthly Donations Report** in **Design View**.

8. Click on the **subform** to select it.

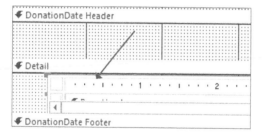

9. Click the **All** tab in the Property Sheet and set the Can Grow and Can Shrink properties to **Yes**.

10. Switch to **Report View** and scroll through the report.

    Notice how the number of donations per month changes and the report shrinks and grows to accommodate the number of donations each month.

Modify the Title

11. Switch to **Design View**.

12. Click the **Monthly Donations Report** title in the Page Header and then click again just in front of *Monthly* to position the insertion point there.

13. Type **Kids for Change** and then press Shift+Enter to force *Monthly Donations Report* to a second line.

14. Click in a blank part of the header and then click the **title** control again to select it.

15. Set the following properties for the title control:

Property	Setting
Width	**4"**
Left	**2"**
Text Align	**Center**

16. Switch to **Print Preview** and scroll through the first page of the report.

Notice more than 1 month appears per page.

17. Use the Navigation bar at the bottom of the window to navigate to Page 2.

Notice the April donations spill over from the previous page. In the next steps, you will insert a page break so that each month begins on a new page.

Insert a Page Break

18. Close Print Preview and then switch to **Design View** and choose **Design→Controls→ Insert Page Break** .

19. Click in the left side of the **DonationDate Footer** section to place the page break there.

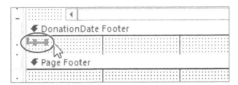

20. Set the Top property of the page break control to **0"**.

21. Click the **DonationDate Footer** section bar and set the Height property to **0.001"**.

This will make the DonationDate Footer section as short as possible so that the page break doesn't push the DonationDate Header down to the next page.

22. Switch to **Print Preview** and use the Navigation bar to navigate through the report pages.

Notice that the donations for each month now start on new pages.

23. Choose **File→Close** to close the database, saving the changes.

Apply Your Skills

Work with Reports and Subreports

In this exercise, you will help Universal Corporate Events, Ltd., create a report that breaks down the company's revenue by venue. You will add a subreport to a main report.

1. Open **A8-A1-UCE** from your **Access Chapter 8** folder and save it as **A8-A1-UCERevised**.

Import a Report

2. Choose **External Data→Import & Link→Access** .
3. Click **Browse** and navigate to your **Access Chapter 8** folder.
4. Choose **A8-A1-UCE–Backup** and click **Open**.
5. Leave the storage setting as Import Tables, Queries, Forms, Reports, Macros, and Modules into the Current Database and click **OK**.
6. Click the **Reports** tab, choose **Venue Revenue Report**, and click **OK**.
7. Leave the Save Import Steps checkbox unchecked and click **Close**.
8. Display the newly imported **Venue Revenue Report** in **Report View**.

   The empty space between the locations is where you will insert the subreport.

Add a Subreport

9. Switch to **Design View** and choose **Design→Controls→Subform/Subreport** .
10. Click in the **VenueID** Header section below the other controls to insert a control and launch the Subreport Wizard.
11. Choose **VenueRevenue Subform** from the Use an Existing Report or Form option and click **Next**.
12. Choose the second linking option (link by VenueID) and click **Next** again.

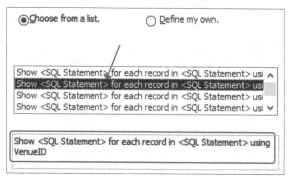

13. Click **Finish** to accept VenueRevenue Subform as the name.

14. Delete the **VenueRevenue Subform** label located just above the subform.

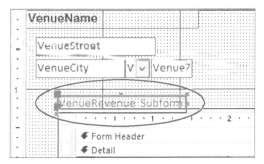

15. Click the new **subform** to select it and set the following properties:

Property	Setting
Width	**7"**
Height	**1.5"**
Top	**1.3"**
Left	**0.25"**
Border Style	**Transparent**

16. Click the **VenueID Header** section bar and set the Height property to **3"**.

17. Switch to **Report View** and scroll through the report.

Each venue now has an event data subform associated with it that contains all of the revenue data for the events.

18. Close the database, saving the changes to the Venue Revenue Report.

APPLY YOUR SKILLS: A8-A2

Create a Report from a Subreport and Number Report Items

In this exercise, you will continue to help Universal Corporate Events, Ltd., create an effective venue revenue report. You will create a report from a subreport and number items on a subreport.

1. Open **A8-A2-UCE** from your **Access Chapter 8** folder and save it as **A8-A2-UCERevised**.

2. Display **Venue Revenue Report** in **Design View**.

3. Right-click the **subreport** and choose **Subreport in New Window**.

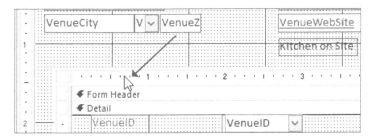

4. Choose **File→Save As→Save Object As→Save As**.

5. Type **VenueRevenue Subreport** as the name, choose **Report** from the Save As drop-down list, and click **OK**.

6. Close **VenueRevenue Subform**.

7. Make sure the subform/subreport is selected and the Property Sheet is displayed.

8. Set the Source Object property on the **All** tab to **Report.VenueRevenue SubReport**.

9. Choose **File→Save** to save the Venue Revenue Report then switch to **Print Preview**.

   The subreport will be displayed.

10. Close **Print Preview** and close the Venue Revenue Report.

Format the Report

Now you will resize the labels and move them from the Detail section into the Report Header section.

11. Display the **VenueRevenue SubReport** in **Design View**.

12. Set the Width property in the Property Sheet to **6"**.

    This will widen the subreport enough to accommodate the changes you are about to make.

13. Use the ⌈Ctrl⌉ key and mouse to select all of the labels and text boxes in both the Detail and Report Footer sections.

14. Click the **Format** tab in the Property Sheet and set the Border Style property to **Transparent** and the Fore Color property to **Black, Text 1.**

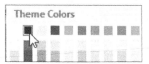

15. Click in an empty part of the form to deselect all controls.

16. Click each label individually and reduce the size to just fit the caption (label text).

17. Click the **Report Header** section bar and set the Height property to **0.3"**.

18. Click the **VenueID** label and choose ⌈Ctrl⌉+⌈X⌉ to cut it.

19. Click in the **Report Header** section, press ⌈Ctrl⌉+⌈V⌉ to paste the label, and then nudge it with the arrow keys, positioning it about **0.25"** in from the left edge.

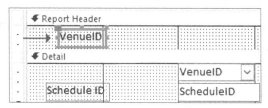

20. Cut and paste the remaining labels from the Detail section into the Report Header using the arrow keys to nudge them until they are aligned approximately as shown.

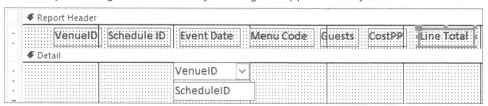

21. Rearrange the Detail section text boxes by dragging them with the mouse, nudging them with the arrow keys, and reducing their widths until they are aligned with the labels in the Report Header approximately as shown here.

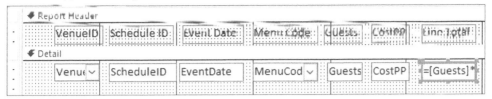

22. Click the **Detail** section bar and set the Height property to **0.3"**.

23. Use the right arrow → key to nudge the calculated control in the Report Footer to the right until it is right-aligned with the Line Total label and the Detail section calculated control as shown here.

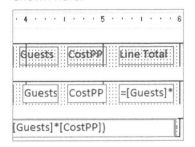

24. Switch to **Layout View** and, if necessary, resize and reposition the controls until they are aligned approximately as shown here and all data is visible.

	VenueID	Schedule ID	Event Date	Menu Code	Guests	CostPP	Line Total
	PalmCt	BRTLuna	10/12/2014	BARSNK	50	$7.50	$375.00
	WMinst	HOLMiller	1/1/2015	CHFBRK	100	$16.00	$1,600.00
	Meadow	HOLMiller	7/2/2014	DESSRT	25	$13.00	$325.00

25. Choose **File→Save** to save the subreport.

Number Report Items

26. Switch to **Design View**.

27. Insert a new text box in the Detail section to the left of the VenueID text box.

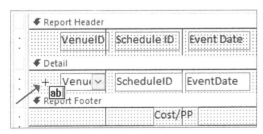

28. Delete the associated label control.

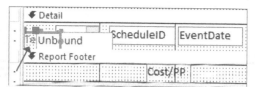

29. Click the new **text box** control and set these property values in the **All** tab of the Property Sheet:

Property	Setting
Name	**txtCount**
Control Source	**=1**
Width	**0.2"**
Top	**0"**
Left	**0"**
Border Style	**Transparent**

30. Click the **Data** tab in the Property Sheet and set the Running Sum property to **Over All**.

31. Select all text boxes in the Detail section and set the top property to **0"**.

32. Save the **VenueRevenue SubReport**.

33. Display the **Venue Revenue Report** in **Print Preview**.

Navigate through the report and notice that the detail lines for each venue are now numbered sequentially.

34. Choose **File→Close** to close the database, saving changes to any reports.

APPLY YOUR SKILLS: A8-A3

Add a Calculated Field and a Page Break

Universal Corporate Events, Ltd., wants to continue to refine its database reports. In this exercise, you will add a field to calculate the total of all the venues' revenues. You will also add a page break to another report to allow each month to begin on a new page.

1. Open **A8-A3-UCE** from your **Access Chapter 8** folder and save it as **A8-A3-UCERevised**.

Add a Calculated Field

2. Display **Venue Revenue Report** in **Report View**.

3. Scroll through the report and notice that each Venue has Line Total calculations and a total of the Line Totals for that venue.

The one thing missing is a grand total at the bottom of the report that sums all the totals for each venue. You will add a calculated control that produces a grand total.

4. Switch to **Design View**.

5. Click the **Report Footer** section bar and set the Height property to **0.4"**.

6. Insert a text box anywhere in the Report Footer section.

7. Select the label for the new text box and set these properties in the Property Sheet Format tab:

Property	Setting
Caption	**Grand Total for All Venues**
Width	**2"**
Top	**0.1"**
Left	**2"**
Font Weight	**Semi-Bold**
Fore Color	**Blue, Accent 1, Darker 50%**

8. Click the new text box and enter these property values in the Property Sheet **All** tab:

Property	Setting
Name	**ActivityCost**
Control Source	**=Sum([Guests]*[ChgPP])**
Format	**Currency**
Width	**1.5"**
Top	**0.1"**
Left	**5"**
Border Style	**Transparent**
Font Weight	**Semi-Bold**
Fore Color	**Blue, Accent 1, Darker 50%**

9. Select the **VenueRevenue Subform** and set both the Can Grow and Can Shrink properties on the Format tab of the Property Sheet to **Yes**.

   This ensures that all venue detail lines will be displayed.

10. Switch to **Report View** and scroll to the end of the report.

    Notice the Grand Total for All Venues *label and the grand total calculated control.*

11. Close Venue Revenue Report, saving the changes.

Insert a Page Break

12. Display the **Event Revenue Report** in **Print Preview**.

13. Scroll through the first page and notice that several months are included on the page.

    The page break you are about to insert will position each month on a separate page.

14. Exit Print Preview and then switch to **Design View** and insert a **Page Break** 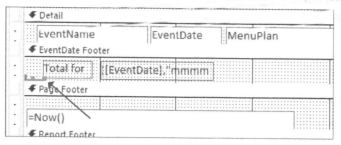 control in the left side of the EventDate Footer just below the *Total for* label.

It's important to position the break below the label, or portions of the report will be cut off.

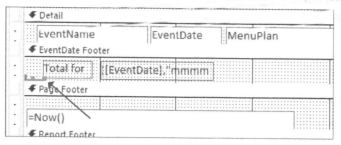

15. Switch to **Print Preview** and notice that just 1 month appears on the first page.

16. Use the Navigation bar to go to the next page and once again just 1 month will be displayed because of the page break.

17. Choose **File→Close** to close the database, saving changes to the Event Revenue Report.

 Extend Your Skills

These exercises challenge you to think critically and apply your new skills. You will be evaluated on your ability to follow directions, completeness, creativity, and the use of proper grammar and mechanics. Save files to your chapter folder. Submit assignments as directed.

A8-E1 That's the Way I See It

You've been asked to modify a database report for the Blue Jean Landscaping database. Open **A8-E1-BJL** and save it as **A8-E1-BJLRevised**. Import the Customer Sales Report from **A8-E1-BJL-Backup**. Add the CustomerSales Subform to the Detail section of the Customer Sales Report.

A8-E2 Be Your Own Boss

As the owner of Blue Jean Landscaping, you want to add more calculations to a report and create page breaks for a more organized viewing of the data. Open **A8-E2-BJL** and save it as **A8-E2-BJLRevised**. Open Customer Sales Report and create a new subreport from the CustomerSales Subform. Calculate the line totals for each subreport line using the formula Price*QtySold. Insert a page break so that each customer will appear on a separate page when you view the report in Print Preview.

A8-E3 Demonstrate Proficiency

The Stormy BBQ Key West store and restaurant is enjoying increased sales, so you must make some changes to the database reports to produce more useful sales results. Open **A8-E3-SBQ** and save it as **A8-E3-SBQRevised**. Import the Merchandise Sales Report from **A8-E3-SBQ-Backup**. Insert the MerchandiseSales Subform into the Detail section of the Merchandise Sales Report to add individual sale line items (choose Show each record in Merchandise using SKU). Save the subform as a report, being sure to close the subform, and then open the new subreport so the changes you make are not reflected in the subform. Calculate each line total (ListPrice*QtySold) in the Detail section of the subreport.

Glossary

action query Performs one of four actions on a group of records (delete, update, append, or create a new table)

append query Query that adds a group of records from one or more sources to the end of one or more tables

Can Grow property Allows the subreport space to expand as necessary so more data appears vertically in the subreport

Cascade Delete Relationship that records in a related table whenever related records in the primary table are deleted

Cascade Update Relationship that updates the value in the key field of a related table when the primary key value in the primary table is changed

delete query Query that deletes a group of records from one or more tables

expression Combination of field names and arithmetic and logical operators required to perform the calculation; an Access formula

group Collection of controls or records that have at least one feature in common; quick forms tie all automatically inserted text boxes and corresponding labels into one group, allowing you to move the entire group but not the individual controls; or, if you want to display all vendors with offices in the same state, you could group on the State field

import The process of retrieving data from other files or applications

index (database) Structure similar to a book index; its main function is to speed up database operations; an index set on key fields uses one or more hidden columns in a table for faster data retrieval

input mask Controls data formats by setting the required characters to display as users enter data, such as slashes (/) for a date field

make table query Query that creates a new table from the selected data in one or more tables

Object Dependencies panel Allows the display of database objects that either use or are used by other objects

parameter query Query that filter records and returns only a subset that matched the value entered, delivering on-the-fly results

referential integrity Relationship protocol that maintains the validity of related data; requires that the data types of related primary and foreign key fields are the same or compatible

smart tags Indicate common actions that may be taken if certain conditions are encountered or if a control has a problem; clicking a smart tag displays a list of possible actions

subform A secondary (child) form placed on a main (parent) form, allowing the user to view and complete data entries for multiple tables through one form

subreport Displays subsets of data derived from related database tables, similar to subforms

update query Query that makes global changes to a group of records in one or more tables

validation rule Field property that enables you to limit values entered into the field to reduce errors associated with data entry (e.g., limit the value typed into an Hours Worked field to less than 60)

validation text Contains instructions or valid data values to help guide the data entry personnel

Index

NOTES

NOTES